D0000607

RADIANCE

Library of Congress Cataloging–in–Publication Data

Underhill, Evelyn, 1875-1941.
    Radiance : a spiritual memoir / of Evelyn Underhill ;
    compiled and edited by Bernard Bangley.
          p.   cm.
    Includes bibliographical references.
      ISBN 1–55725–355–2 (pbk.)
      1. Spiritual life—Christianity. I. Bangley, Bernard, 1935-
    II. Title.
      BV4501.3.U53 2004
      248.2'2'092—dc22

                                                      2003027025

10 9 8 7 6 5 4 3 2 1

© 2004 by Bernard Bangley

ISBN 1-55725-355-2

Published by Paraclete Press
Brewster, Massachusetts
www.paracletepress.com

Printed in the United States of America.

Evelyn Underhill
(1875-1941)

Evelyn Underhill was a gifted spiritual writer, novelist, and poet, who published more than thirty books including her pivotal work, *Mysticism*, published in 1911. Underhill became the Upton Lecturer in the Philosophy of Religion at Manchester College in 1921 and was the first woman to give a series of lectures on theology at Oxford.

Bernard Bangley has authored and edited numerous books, including *Christian Classics in Modern English*, *Talks on the Song of Songs by Bernard of Clairvaux*, and *Rooted in Faith: Meditations from the Reformers*. A retired Presbyterian minister, Mr. Bangley lives in Virginia.

CONTENTS

FOUR
mature insight
1932-1941

INTRODUCTION

Evelyn Underhill (1875–1941) was a gifted British spiritual writer, the author of more than thirty books. Without formal religious or theological education, she uncovered and popularized a vast treasure of Christian mystical literature.

This book is a unique compilation of her work. It contains selections from the full spectrum of her writing—both public and private, from her youth to the end of her life. Some of this material is now out of print. Each excerpt has been included as an illustration of the progress of her personal spiritual development.

As consciousness of our own spirituality grows in us, it can be extremely helpful to observe how it has worked out in other lives. Evelyn Underhill is an ideal choice for such a study. She read more widely than most of us, had an authentic mystical experience, and refused to distort such activity by putting herself at the center. Her focus was upon God rather than herself. Mysticism was not, for her, something odd, but entirely natural. It had nothing to do with popular occult practices. She noticed that the classical mystics were not self-centered, but God-centered. There is a balanced sanity in her work.

A *Spectator* review of one of her books said there is something infectious about her "style with its deep rooted common sense, its virile idiom, and its creaturely appreciation of the beauty of the world. These addresses will bear reading and rereading, for they are the fruits of a life that is all too rare in this day and age." That life may be clearly perceived in Evelyn Underhill's writing even when she does not intend it to be autobiographical. Who can doubt that her rarely seen early novel *The Gray World* gives us a glimpse into her own childhood? Her early spiritual awareness and the resulting stresses are evident in the passages included here. The poetry of her youth demonstrates her spiritual sensitivity and her deep sympathy for others.

Underhill's *Mysticism* is a classic in a heavy academic style, and yet, in the portions included in this volume, we may derive a glimpse of the early curiosity that resulted from her strong spiritual consciousness. With the exception of one poem and the final excerpt from an essay, all selections are printed in chronological order, allowing the alert reader to see the internal activity of God's spirit across Underhill's lifetime.

There is an obvious change that takes place between her work on *Mysticism* in 1907 and the first retreat she conducted in 1924. Even her style and choice of words turn a corner. Her expression of the spiritual life takes on a deeper, warmer color. Her understanding of the importance of Christ becomes more prominent. There is a deeper awareness of the spiritual needs of her readers.

A unique contribution of this compilation is that it permits us to see the contrast and continuity between Evelyn Underhill's published writing and her private journaling. Including personal correspondence and passages from her notebooks allows us to see beyond the veil that protects most authors. This compilation honestly presents the extraordinary personal and spiritual struggle of Evelyn Underhill. Here is something genuine.

We should not overlook this brilliant laywoman's accomplishment. Much as Felix Mendelssohn was responsible for the revival of public interest in the neglected music of J. S. Bach, Evelyn Underhill introduced Protestant Christians to the forgotten writers of medieval Catholic spirituality. She had found and read obscure works that would not be released in definitive translations until after her groundbreaking effort.

Because of this work the Church and academia quickly recognized Underhill as a leading authority on classical mysticism. She became something of a celebrity. In 1921 she was invited to be the Upton Lecturer in Philosophy of Religion at Manchester College. As a knowledgeable and articulate speaker, Underhill also became the first woman to give a series of lectures on theology at Oxford, the first woman to lecture to clergy in the Church of England, the first woman to lead spiritual retreats, and the first woman to encourage ecumenical links between separated churches.

Fluent in several languages, solidly familiar with the classics, well read in both current theology and the vast literature of Western spirituality, she continued to gain respect as a competent writer and speaker. One admirer commented, "As you listened you asked yourself, Oxford or Cambridge? And then realized with a start that she was for the most part self-taught, and that though she owed a certain amount to the start and trend that King's College had given to her studies, she owed most to her unwearied zest for the truth, to her admiring love of sanctity, her diligent and enthusiastic study."

Evelyn Underhill was the only child of Sir Arthur Underhill. She grew up in an essentially secular environment, among yachts and tea parties. Of her childhood, she writes, "I was not brought up to religion." Her spiritual quest orig- inated independently of her home. The combination of a quick mind and a sensitive soul led her to investigate matters on her own, beginning at an early age.

Her investigations led her to participate in public worship at both Anglican and Catholic churches. In the early 1900s she decided to spend a week, with a friend, in Southampton at St. Mary of the Angels, a convent of Franciscan nuns. She was able to endure only four days of "perpetual prayer," but she reported it affected her deeply. "The day after I came away, a good deal shaken but unconvinced, I was 'converted' quite suddenly once and for all by an overpowering vision which had really no specific Christian element but yet convinced me that the Catholic religion was true."

A prominent Catholic writer, Baron von Hügel, read her big book on mysticism and began to correspond with her. In 1919 he became her spiritual director. This relationship was lasting and beneficial to both for the remaining five years of von Hügel's life.

Baron von Hügel discouraged Evelyn from becoming a Catholic and advised her to follow her husband's wishes. She had recently married Hubert Stuart Moore, a successful barrister who encouraged her to officially unite with the Anglican Church. Her marriage produced no children, but she kept many cats, and considered her spiritual friends as "family." Her friends report that she enjoyed her London home life, and was witty, bright, and curious. She was a gardener and an expert bookbinder who enjoyed sailing and motorcycle riding with her husband. We also know that Evelyn appreciated good art and relished high mountains.

Then, during 1923 and 1924, Evelyn Underhill experienced a profound spiritual struggle, something none of her friends or family suspected. The sick mother she had nursed so tenderly died. Baron von Hügel also died. In her grief, she became extraordinarily critical of herself, believing her ego stood in the way of a desire to be more useful to God. She lost all taste for spiritual bluebirds and rainbows. She sought no divine consolations. What she felt God wanted of her was sacrificial commitment.

The grand theme that emerges as her writing progresses through these stressful years is the human response to God's grace. "We love because he first loved us." (1 John 4:19 NIV). As she worked through her grief, an awareness of God's transcendence and perfection developed steadily. The spiritual life, after all, is not a series of mystical experiences such as rapture and ecstasy, visions and locutions. Such things may happen, but they are not vital to the spiritual life. What matters is a reverent awakening to God. A Christian mystic, such as Evelyn Underhill, does not look for anything personal—no spiritual intoxication. The mystic's goal is self-surrender.

The truth is, Evelyn Underhill was having mystical experiences. Her notebooks and some of her correspondence are the only references available. She felt as though she were "an almost invisible speck in the Ocean" of God's reality. She was aware of "the interpenetration of Spirit," "we in Christ and He in us." She heard "the Voice." Extraordinary moments such as these did not cause her to feel superior or privileged. Rather, they increased her sense of inadequacy, causing tension and anxiety. Her private journal entries reveal her doubts and failures as well as her understanding of the accepting love of God. When these passages of personal mystical experience are read together with passages from her books, we gain insight into the depth of her spiritual awareness. There can be no doubt of her sincerity. She not only wrote and spoke about the spiritual life—she also lived it.

This volume presents her writing with only the slightest alterations. Her language cannot, and should not, be separated from her times. A few tweaks of early twentieth-century British syntax, spelling, punctuation, and vocabulary are the only changes in these full excerpts of her work. Editorial inconsistencies and typographical errors sometimes mar existing volumes of her titles. We have corrected these. Her many footnotes have also been eliminated: These sources are not readily available today and would be of little help to the modern reader.

The intention of this text is to be a short guide to Evelyn Underhill's spiritual development, using firsthand material. Preparing it resulted in many startling moments of agreement and wonder. It is my wish that as you read, you will be flooded with similar insight and understanding of the ways of God with the human soul.

early writings

1892-1914

Personal Diary
1892

The Eve of Her 17th Birthday

Diary, December 5, 1892

I am going to write down this short account of my own feelings and opinions because I think that tomorrow will close a period of my life, and I want to preserve some memory of it before it quite goes away.

First as to ideals. My ideal of a man is that he should be true, strong, intellectual, and considerate; not an adherent of any extreme party, but always ready to help the poor and oppressed. It does not matter if he is not good-looking or is shy or brusque, for those are outside things. I have never read or seen a man who comes up to my ideal. In real life I most admire Mahomet, because he was sincere, Giordano Bruno, because he was strong for the truth, and Jesus Christ because ethically He was perfect, and always thought of the weak ones first.

In fiction, I admire Milton's Satan for his strength, Tennyson's King Arthur for his goodness, and Shakespeare's Romeo for his personal charms.

My ideal of a woman is that she should be clever, vivacious, accurately but not priggishly informed, gentle, truthful, tactful, and tolerant, and should have a due sense of proportion. I have never met or read of anyone exactly like this, but in real life my own mother comes nearest to it. I think in fiction, Angela Messenger in All Sorts and Conditions of Men.

My favorite heroines in real life are Joan of Arc for her sincerity, and Caroline Herschel for her unselfish love of knowledge. In fiction I like Hypatia, Portia, and Princess Ida, for their mental qualities, Milton's Eve for her womanliness, and Angela Messenger for herself.

My favorite prose writers are Matthew Arnold, Hallam, and Huxley for their style, Carlyle for his Philosophy, Besant for his characters. Among the poets I prefer Shakespeare for general excellence, Milton for majesty, Tennyson and Keats for beautiful thoughts, musically set, and Calverley and Austin Dobson for *vers de société*.

Among animals I prefer the cat, because when off duty in a zoological capacity it makes an excellent muff.

In politics I am a Socialist. I think it is the only fair form of government, and it gives every class an equal status, and does away with the incentive to many sorts of crime.

As to religion, I don't quite know, except that I believe in a God, and think it is better to love and help the poor people round me than to go on saying that I love an abstract Spirit whom I have never seen. If I can do both, all the better, but it is best to begin with the nearest. I do not think anything is gained by being orthodox, and a great deal of the beauty and sweetness of things is lost by being bigoted and dogmatic. If we are to see God at all it must be through nature and our fellow men. Science holds a lamp up to heaven, not down to the Churches.

I don't believe in worrying God with prayers for things we want. If He is omnipotent He knows we want them, and if He isn't, He can't give them to us. I think it is an insult to Him to repeat the same prayers every day. It is as much as to say He is deaf, or very slow of comprehension. . . .

Goodbye sixteen years old. I hope my mind will not grow tall to look down on things, but wide to embrace all sorts of things. . . .

The Gray World

1904

Evelyn Underhill expressed some of her early ideas in novels, the first of which was The Gray World. *While it does not succeed as a novel, it has a distinct character that sets it apart from ordinary fiction. For the observant reader it is clearly a report of the inner life of a young mystic. Whether consciously or unconsciously, Evelyn has given us a thinly concealed autobiography, written from personal experience. Included are such things as her travels in Italy, her skill in bookbinding, her sailing expeditions, and her mental prodding under every spiritual stone. The explorations she describes are familiar to any spiritually alert person in the third decade of life. The central character appears to be a blending of the reported youthful experiences of William Blake and her own experience. It is but a short step from her hero's rather plain first name, Willie, to William Blake, whom she elsewhere declares to be "almost alone amongst English Protestant mystics." There is little doubt that she found much in her own experience that resonated harmonically with Blake. The short excerpt that follows gives clear insight into the struggles of her youthful spiritual awareness. A longer excerpt is included in an appendix.*

From *The Gray World*

Most children of the normal type have their moments of mysticism, when their spirit first stirs and they wonder what they really are. . . . Master Hopkinson, always acutely conscious of two worlds equally near to him, pondered perhaps less on these things, because to him they were so obvious, objectionable, and distinct. . . .

The Gray World was the warp on which the bright threads of his sensuous existence were spread. . . . This sudden discovery that the rest of the family did not share his knowledge, live the same dual life, or frequent the same dim country, startled and distressed him. . . .

He got the habit of looking into every book that he could find, for he had somehow acquired the idea that books were real, though people, he knew, were not. One day, he found a thin volume of verse, left probably by some chance visitor. . . . This book Willie opened, and read, among much unintelligible loveliness, the following quatrain:

> "We are no other than a moving row
> Of Magic Shadow-shapes that come and go
> Round with the Sun-illumined Lantern held
> In Midnight by the Master of the Show."

"Then there is some one else who knows!" he thought; and went away companioned and less lonely for that knowledge. . . .

꙲

Stephen and Willie . . . were little bound by the limitations of their elders. Each obtained early, if vague, assurance of the other's interest in spiritual things, and bridges were soon established between them. . . .

Stephen argued his way toward the light by intellectual effort; did not perceive as Willie did, naturally and irrationally, the Gray World folded in the shadow-world of sense. . . . He wished to know the beyond as children wish to see fairies, because he believed it to be strange, beautiful, exciting.

They went together fairly regularly to the meetings of the Searchers of the Soul . . . [On] an evening in which the tone of the meeting had been one of great intellectual as well as atmospheric stuffiness . . . Willie and Stephen, escaping at last . . . stood upon the threshold, amazed and comforted by

the purity which the west wind blows from a dark sky. . . .
The moon rode high above London. . . . Under that heaven,
so secret and so white, one seemed to imagine wide spaces of
quiet and happy country at rest; and the black shadow of
London—man's ugly attempt to build himself a world—lying
like a blot in the midst, yet sharing in the same merciful
dispensation of darkness and light. . . .

"On a night like this," said Stephen, "so magical and still,
one is almost tempted to wonder if anything is real. These
streets aren't the same streets now—their essence isn't the
same—as in daytime. And who's to say which is the real
street?"

"It's we who are different," said Willie. "And so we see
another world. . . ."

"Oh," said Stephen, suddenly and violently. "Look! Look
at the wonder and the mystery of it all! The great stars and
the darkness; and the strange, careless, cruel earth. It must be
different really; more ordered, more sane. Will one ever find
the thing itself?"

"Better not. You're happiest in the searching. . . ."

⊸囚

[Willie] felt himself to be, not any more the man in the
world, but the pilgrim soul, footing it between the stars. He
was walking alone, sturdily self-dependent, through exquisite
landscape toward an appointed goal. That, surely, should be
his life. That *was* life—a journey upon the great highway of
the world toward an abiding city. A journey to be taken
joyfully and in gratitude because of the beauty of the road.

He conceived now of the world, of the body, as
momentary conditions in the infinite progress of the spirit.
Used rightly, a discipline, an initiation; used wrongly, a peril
whose deeps he had once known. His idealism had come to
this; to a guarded, tolerant acquiescence in the queer distorting

medium of his senses, a willingness within limits to accept their reports. But it was the holy, the beautiful aspect of things that he asked them to show him. That was significant, true. No illusion of time and space, but an eternal thing which it was the very business of matter to shadow forth, the duty of that pilgrim soul in him to apprehend. . . .

Willie was beginning to recover from the disease of spiritual self-seeking, which had crippled his first years. He had seen, at last, the face of the Great Companion. He knew what he wanted: the constant presence of that mysterious guide, the constant assurance of a strange but enduring amity. He had come to the second, or illuminative, stage of the journey; for his way, after all, had been the old mystic's way. There is no other practicable path for those who are determined on reality, who have found out the gigantic deception we accept as the visible world, the gigantic foolishness of our comfortable common sense.

The old formula came back to his mind: "Purgation, illumination, contemplation"—the three stages of the Via Mystica, acknowledged by all the masters who had trod it, the explorers who had left notes of its geography behind. This trinity of experience seemed to co-relate in some way with the triune vision of reality—"The triple star of goodness, truth, and beauty"—promised to those who attained its highest stage. In his wanderings, apparently so devious, he had followed the old lines very exactly. . . .

Looking into the depths of the woods, . . . nothing is easier than to believe in nymphs, dryads, elemental presences of the forest. They stand shadowy upon the paths; they laugh and sigh; and sometimes the soul hears them with a sudden terror. . . . In such a way the voices of the woods spoke to Mr. Willie Hopkinson as he trod a path between the trees. He gave them a willing attention. He had developed the sense of adventure, that power which differentiates the romantic from the prosaic world. He felt that everything was possible, and to one who is in this disposition the impossible is sure to come.

Want of faith in the improbable is really responsible for all that is deliberately dreary in our lives. Those who go whistling down the road, eyes raised to the sun and hope waiting round the corner, seldom find the excursion of a life a disappointing one.

Mysticism

1910

Evelyn Underhill finished her "big book" in her thirty-fifth year.
Mysticism *received immediate attention and established the author as a
rare authority on what her contemporaries considered an obscure and precarious subject. She had uncovered and read a remarkably vast collection
of classic literature on spirituality, as may be seen in her bibliography. The
depth and authenticity of her research, coupled with a manner of expression
that assures the reader she is in command of her subject, disarmed and
impressed hesitant skeptics. The book is written in a careful academic style
within a broad and sweeping logical outline. Few candidates for a PhD
have ever submitted a dissertation that exhibits such superior scholarship.*

In the preface to the first edition she writes: "Those mystics,
properly speaking, can only be studied in their works: works
which are for the most part left unread by those who now talk
much about mysticism. Certainly the general reader has this
excuse, that the masterpieces of mystical literature, full of
strange beauties though they be, offer considerable difficulties
to those who come to them unprepared."

She further acknowledges that the term "Mysticism" is "one of the
most abused words in the English language. It has been used
in different and often mutually exclusive senses by religion,
poetry, and philosophy: has been claimed as an excuse for
every kind of occultism, for dilute transcendentalism, vapid
symbolism, religious or aesthetic sentimentality, and bad
metaphysics."

*Twenty years after its original publication, Evelyn expressed her own
criticism of the work, saying she would state things differently.* "More

emphasis would be given (*a*) to the concrete, richly living yet unchanging character of the Reality over against the mystic, as the first term, cause, and incentive of his experience; (*b*) to that paradox of utter contrast yet profound relation between the Creator and the creature, God and the soul, which makes possible his development; (*c*) to the predominant part played in that development by the free and prevenient action of the Supernatural—in theological language, by 'grace'—as against all merely evolutionary or emergent theories of spiritual transcendence."

When she acknowledges that during the two decades that followed the publication of Mysticism *there were tremendous advances in both understanding and in the careful editing of original texts, she does not claim any credit. There can be little doubt that her personal effort acted as a catalyst, spurring on the studies of others.*

From *Mysticism*

The mystics show us an independent spiritual life, a fruition of the Absolute, enjoyed with a fullness to which others cannot attain. They are the heroic examples of the life of spirit, as the great artists, the great discoverers, are the heroic examples of the life of beauty and the life of truth. Directly participating, like all artists, in the Divine Life, they are usually persons of great vitality: but this vitality expresses itself in unusual forms, hard of understanding for ordinary men. When we see a picture or a poem, hear a musical composition, we accept it as an expression of life, an earnest of the power which brought it forth. But the deep contemplations of the great mystic, his visionary reconstructions of reality, and the fragments of them which he is able to report, do not seem to us—as they are—the equivalents, or more often the superiors of the artistic and scientific achievements of other great men.

Mysticism, then, offers us the history, as old as civilization, of a race of adventurers who have carried to its term the process of a deliberate and active return to the divine fount of things. They have surrendered themselves to the life-movement of the universe, hence have lived with an intenser life than other men can ever know; have transcended the "sense-world" in order to live on high levels the spiritual life. Therefore they witness to all that our latent spiritual con-sciousness, which shows itself in the "hunger for the Absolute," can be made to mean to us if we develop it; and have in this respect a unique importance for the race. It is the mystics, too, who have perfected that method of intuition, that knowledge by union, the existence of which philosophy has been driven to acknowledge. But where the metaphysician obtains at best a sidelong glance at that Being "unchanging yet elusive," whom he has so often defined but never discovered, the artist a brief and dazzling vision of the Beauty which is Truth, [mystics] gaze with confidence into the very eyes of the Beloved.

The mystics, again, are, by their very constitution, acutely conscious of the free and active "World of Becoming," the Divine Immanence and its travail. It is in them and they are in it; or, as they put it in their blunt theological way, "the Spirit of God is within you." But they are not satisfied with this statement and this knowledge; and here it is that they part company with vitalism. It is, they think, but half a truth. To know Reality in this way, to know it in its dynamic aspect, to enter into "the great life of the All": this is indeed, in the last resort, to know it supremely from the point of view of man—to liberate from selfhood the human consciousness— but it is not to know it from the point of view of God. There are planes of being beyond this, countries dark to the intellect, deeps into which only the very greatest contemplatives have looked. These, coming forth, have declared with Ruysbroeck that "God according to the Persons is Eternal Work, but according to the Essence and Its perpetual stillness He is Eternal Rest."

The full spiritual consciousness of the true mystic is developed not in one, but in two apparently opposite but really complementary directions:

". . . io vidi
Ambo le corti del ciel manifeste."

[. . . I saw both of the Courts of Heaven made manifest. (From Dante's *Paradiso*, canto XXX.)]

On the one hand he is intensely aware of, and knows himself to be at one with that active World of Becoming, that immanent Life, from which his own life takes its rise. Hence, though he has broken forever with the bondage of the senses, he perceives in every manifestation of life a sacramental meaning; a loveliness, a wonder, a heightened significance, which is hidden from other men. He may, with St. Francis, call the Sun and the Moon, Water and Fire, his brothers and his sisters: or receive, with Blake, the message of the trees. Because of his cultivation of disinterested love, because his outlook is not conditioned by "the exclusive action of the will-to-live," he has attained the power of communion with the living reality of the universe; and in this respect he can truly say that he finds "God in all and all in God." Thus, the skilled spiritual vision of Lady Julian, transcending the limitations of human perception, entering into harmony with a larger world whose rhythms cannot be received by common men, *saw* the all-enfolding Divine Life, the mesh of reality. "For as the body is clad in the cloth," she said, "and the flesh in the skin and the bones in the flesh and the heart in the whole, so are we, soul and body, clad in the Goodness of God and enclosed. Yea, and the more homely: for all these may waste and wear away, but the Goodness of God is ever whole." Many mystical poets and pantheistic mystics never pass beyond this degree of lucidity.

On the other hand, the full mystic consciousness also attains to what is, I think, its really characteristic quality. It develops the power of apprehending the Absolute, Pure Being, the utterly Transcendent: or, as its possessor would say, it can experience "passive union with God." This all-round expansion of consciousness, with its dual power of knowing by communion the temporal and eternal, immanent and transcendent aspects of reality—the life of the All, vivid, flowing and changing, and the changeless, conditionless life of the One—is the peculiar mark, the *ultimo sigillo* [ultimate seal] of the great mystic, and must never be forgotten in studying his life and work.

As the ordinary man is the meeting-place between two stages of reality—the sense-world and the world of the spiritual life—so the mystic, standing head and shoulders above ordinary men, is again the meeting-place between two orders. Or, if you like it better, he is able to perceive and react to reality under two modes. On the one hand he knows, and rests in, the eternal world of Pure Being, the "Sea Pacific" of the Godhead, indubitably present to him in his ecstasies, attained by him in the union of love. On the other, he knows—and works in—that "stormy sea," the vital World of Becoming which is the expression of Its will. "Illuminated men," says Ruysbroeck, "are caught up, above the reason, into naked vision. There the Divine Unity dwells and calls them. Hence their bare vision, cleansed and free, penetrates the activity of all created things, and pursues it to search it out even to its height."

Though philosophy has striven since thought began—and striven in vain—to resolve the paradox of Being and Becoming, of Eternity and Time, she has failed strangely enough to perceive that a certain type of personality has substituted experience for her guesses at truth; and achieved its solution, not by the dubious processes of thought, but by direct perception. To the great mystic the "problem of the Absolute" presents itself in terms of life, not in terms of dialectic. He solves it in terms of life: by a change or growth of consciousness which—thanks to his peculiar genius—enables him to apprehend that two-fold Vision of Reality which eludes the perceptive powers of other men.

It is extraordinary that this fact of experience—a central fact for the understanding of the contemplative type—has received so little attention from writers upon mysticism. As we proceed with our inquiry, its importance, its far-reaching implications in the domains of psychology, of theology, of action, will become more and more evident. It provides the reason why the mystics could never accept the diagram of the Vitalists or Evolutionists as a complete statement of the nature of Reality. "Whatever be the limits of your knowledge, we know"—they would say—"that the world has another aspect than this: the aspect which is present to the mind of God." "Tranquility according to His essence, activity according to His nature: perfect stillness, perfect fecundity," says Ruysbroeck again, this is the two-fold character of the Absolute. That which to us is action, to Him, they declare, is rest; "His very peace and stillness coming from the brimming fullness of His infinite life." That which to us is Many, to that Transcendent Knower is One. Our World of Becoming rests on the bosom of that Pure Being which has ever been the final Object of man's quest: the "river in which we cannot bathe twice" is the stormy flood of life flowing toward that divine sea. "How glorious," says the Voice of the Eternal to St. Catherine of Siena, "is that soul which has indeed been able to pass from the stormy ocean to Me, the Sea Pacific, and in that Sea, which is Myself, to fill the pitcher of her heart."

The evolution of the mystic consciousness, then, brings its possessors to this transcendent point of view: their secret is this unity in diversity, this stillness in strife. Here they are in harmony with Heraclitus rather than with his modern interpreters. That most mystical of philosophers discerned a hidden unity beneath the battle, transcending all created opposites; and taught his disciples that "Having hearkened not unto me but unto the Logos, it is wise to confess that all things are *one.*" This is the secret at which the idealists' arid concept of Pure Being has tried, so timidly, to hint: and which the Vitalists' more intimate, more actual concept of Becoming has tried, so unnecessarily, to destroy. We shall see the glorious raiment in which the Christian mystics deck it when we come to consider their theological map of the quest.

If it be objected—and this objection has been made by advocates of each school of thought—that the existence of the idealists' and mystics' "Absolute" is utterly inconsistent with the deeply alive, striving life which the Vitalists identify with reality, I reply that both concepts at bottom are but symbols of realities which the human mind can never reach: and that the idea of stillness, unity and peace is and has ever been humanity's best translation of its intuition of the achieved Perfection of God. "In the midst of silence a hidden world was spoken to me. Where is this Silence, and where is the place in which this word is spoken? It is in the purest that the soul can produce, in her noblest part, in the Ground, even the Being of the Soul." So Eckhart: and here he does but subscribe to a universal tradition. The mystics have always insisted that "Be still, be still, and *know*" is the condition of man's purest and most direct apprehension of reality: that he experiences in quiet the truest and deepest activity: and Christianity when she formulated her philosophy made haste to adopt and express this paradox.

Now in persons of mystical genius, the qualities which the stress of normal life tends to keep below the threshold of consciousness are of enormous strength. In these natural explorers of Eternity the "transcendental faculty," the "eye of the soul," is not merely present in embryo, but is highly developed; and is combined with great emotional and volitional power. The result of the segregation of such qualities below the threshold of consciousness is to remove from them the friction of those counter-balancing traits in the surface mind with which they might collide. They are "in the hiddenness," as Jacob Boehme would say. There they develop unchecked, until a point is reached at which their strength is such that they break their bounds and emerge into the conscious field: either temporarily dominating the subject as in ecstasy, or permanently transmuting the old self, as in the "unitive life." The attainment of this point may be accelerated by processes which have always been known and valued by the mystics, and which tend to produce a state of consciousness classed by psychologists with dreams, reverie, and the results of hypnosis. In all these the normal surface-consciousness is deliberately or involuntarily lulled, the images and ideas connected with normal life are excluded, and images or faculties from "beyond the threshold" are able to take their place.

Of course these images or faculties may or may not be more valuable than those already present in the surface-consciousness. In the ordinary subject, often enough, they are but the odds and ends for which the superficial mind has found no use. In the mystic, they are of a very different order: and this fact justifies the means which he instinctively employs to secure their emergence. Indian mysticism founds its external system almost wholly on (a) asceticism, the domination of the senses, and (b) the deliberate practice of self-hypnosis; either by fixing the eyes on a near object, or by the rhythmic repetition of the *mantra* or sacred word. By these complementary forms of discipline, the pull of the phenomenal world is diminished and the mind is placed at the disposal of the subconscious powers. Dancing, music, and other exaggerations of natural rhythm have been pressed into the same service by the Greek initiates of Dionysus, by the Gnostics, by innumerable other mystic cults. That these proceedings do effect a remarkable change in the human consciousness is proved experience, though how and why they do it is as yet little understood.

Such artificial and deliberate production of ecstasy is against the whole instinct of the Christian contemplatives; but here and there among them also we find instances in which ecstatic trance or lucidity, the liberation of the "transcendental sense," was inadvertently produced by purely physical means. Thus Jacob Boehme, the "Teutonic theosopher," having one day as he sat in his room "gazed fixedly upon a burnished pewter dish which reflected the sunshine with great brilliance," fell into an inward ecstasy, and it seemed to him as if he could look into the principles and deepest foundations of things. The contemplation of running water had the same effect on St. Ignatius Loyola. Sitting on the bank of a river one day, and facing the stream, which was running deep, "the eyes of his mind were opened, not so as to see any kind of vision, but so as to understand and comprehend spiritual things . . . and this with such clearness that for him all these things were made new." This method of attaining to mental lucidity by a narrowing and simplification of the conscious field, finds an apt parallel in the practice of Immanuel Kant, who "found that he could better engage in philosophical thought while *gazing steadily* at a neighboring church steeple."

It need hardly be said that rationalistic writers, ignoring the parallels offered by the artistic and philosophic tempera-ments, have seized eagerly upon the evidence afforded by such instances of apparent mono-ideism and self-hypnosis in the lives of the mystics, and by the physical disturbances which accompany the ecstatic trance, and sought by its application to attribute all the abnormal perceptions of contemplative genius to hysteria or other disease. They have not hesitated to call St. Paul an epileptic and St. Teresa the "patron saint of hysterics," and have found room for most of their spiritual kindred in various departments of the pathological museum. They have been helped in this grateful task by the acknowledged fact that the great contemplatives, though almost always persons of robust intelligence and marked practical or intellectual ability—Plotinus, St. Bernard, the two Saints Catherine, St. Teresa, St. John of the Cross, and the Sufi poets Jàmi and Jalalu'ddin are cases in point—have often suffered from bad physical health. More, their mystical activities have generally reacted upon their bodies in a definite and special way, producing in several cases a particular kind of illness and of physical disability, accompanied by pains and functional disturbances for which no organic cause could be discovered, unless that cause were the immense strain which exalted spirit puts upon a body which is adapted to a very different form of life.

It is certain that the abnormal and highly sensitized type of mind which we call mystical does frequently, but not always, produce or accompany strange and inexplicable modifications of the physical organism with which it is linked. The supernatural is not here in question, except in so far as we are inclined to give that name to natural phenomena which we do not understand. Such instances of psycho-physical parallelism as the stigmatizations of the saints—and indeed of other suggestible subjects hardly to be ranked as saints— will occur to anyone. I here offer to the reader another less discussed and more extraordinary example of the modifying influence of the spirit on the supposed "laws" of bodily life.

We know, as a historical fact, unusually well attested by contemporary evidence and quite outside the sphere of

hagiographic romance, that both St. Catherine of Siena and
her namesake St. Catherine of Genoa—active women as well
as ecstatics, the first a philanthropist, reformer, and politician,
the second an original theologian and for many years the
highly efficient matron of a large hospital—lived, in the first
case for years, in the second for constantly repeated periods
of many weeks, without other food than the consecrated
Host which they received at Holy Communion. They did
this, not by way of difficult obedience to a pious vow, but
because they could not live in any other way. While fasting,
they were well and active, capable of dealing with the
innumerable responsibilities which filled their lives. But the
attempt to eat even a few mouthfuls—and this attempt was
constantly repeated, for, like all true saints, they detested
eccentricity—at once made them ill and had to be abandoned
as useless.

In spite of the researches of Murisier, Janet, Ribot, and
other psychologists, and their persevering attempts to find a
pathological explanation which will fit all mystic facts, this
and other marked physical peculiarities which accompany
the mystical temperament belong as yet to the unsolved
problems of humanity. They need to be removed both from
the sphere of marvel and from that of disease—into which
enthusiastic friends and foes force them by turn—to the
sphere of pure psychology; and there studied dispassionately
with the attention which we so willingly bestow on the less
interesting eccentricities of degeneracy and vice. Their
existence no more discredits the sanity of mysticism or the
validity of its results than the unstable nervous condition
usually noticed in artists—who share to some extent the
mystic's apprehension of the Real—discredits art. "In such
cases as Kant and Beethoven," says Von Hügel justly, "a
classifier of humanity according to its psycho-physical
phenomena alone would put these great discoverers and

creators, without hesitation, among hopeless and useless hypochondriacs."

In the case of the mystics and the disease of hysteria, with its astounding variety of mental symptoms, its strange power of disintegrating, rearranging, and enhancing the elements of consciousness, its tendencies to automatism and ecstasy, has been most often invoked to provide an explanation of the observed phenomena. This is as if one sought the source of the genius of Taglioni in the symptoms of St. Vitus's dance. Both the art and the disease have to do with bodily movements. So too both mysticism and hysteria have to do with the domination of consciousness by one fixed and intense idea or intuition, which rules the life and is able to produce amazing physical and psychical results. In the hysteric patient this idea is often trivial or morbid but has become—thanks to the self's unstable mental condition—an obsession. In the mystic the dominant idea is a great one: so great in fact, that when it is received in its completeness by the human consciousness, almost of necessity it ousts all else. It is nothing less than the idea of perception of the transcendent reality and presence of God. Hence the mono-ideism of the mystic is rational, while that of the hysteric patient is invariably irrational.

On the whole then, while psycho-physical relations remain so little understood, it would seem more prudent, and certainly more scientific, to withhold our judgment on the meaning of the psycho-physical phenomena which accompany the mystic life, instead of basing destructive criticism on facts which are avowedly mysterious and at least capable of more than one interpretation. To deduce the nature of a compound from the character of its by-products is notoriously unsafe.

Our bodies are animal things, made for animal activities. When a spirit of unusual ardor insists on using its nerve-cells for other activities, they kick against the pricks and inflict, as the mystics themselves acknowledge, the penalty of "mystical ill-health." "Believe me, children," says Tauler, "one who would know much about these high matters would often have to keep his bed, for his bodily frame could not support it." "I cause thee extreme pain of body," says the voice of Love to Mechthild of Magdeburg. "If I gave myself to thee as often as thou wouldst have me, I should deprive myself of the sweet shelter I have of thee in this world, for a thousand bodies could not protect a loving soul from her desire. Therefore the higher the love the greater the pain."

On the other hand the exalted personality of the mystic—his self-discipline, his heroic acceptance of labor and suffering, and his inflexible will—raises to a higher term that normal power of mind over body which all possess. Also the contemplative state—like the hypnotic state in a healthy person—seems to enhance life by throwing open deeper levels of personality. The self then drinks at a fountain which is fed by the Universal Life. True ecstasy is notoriously life-enhancing. In it a bracing contact with Reality seems to take place, and as a result the subject is himself more real. Often, says St. Teresa, even the sick come forth from ecstasy healthy and with new strength; for something great is then given to the soul. Contact has been set up with levels of being which the daily routine of existence leaves untouched. Hence the extraordinary powers of endurance, and independence of external conditions, which the great ecstatics so often display.

If we see in the mystics, as some have done, the sporadic beginning of a power, a higher consciousness, towards which the race slowly tends, then it seems likely enough that where it appears nerves and organs should suffer under a stress to which they have not yet become adapted, and that a spirit more highly organized than its bodily home should be able to impose strange conditions on the flesh. When man first stood upright, a body long accustomed to go on all fours, legs which had adjusted themselves to bearing but half his weight, must have rebelled against this unnatural proceeding, inflicting upon its author much pain and discomfort if not absolute illness. It is at least permissible to look upon the strange "psycho-physical" state common among the mystics as just such a rebellion on the part of a normal nervous and vascular system against the exigencies of a way of life to which it has not yet adjusted itself.

In spite of such rebellion, and of the tortures to which it has subjected them, the mystics, oddly enough, are a long-lived race: an awkward fact for critics of the physiological school. To take only a few instances from among marked ecstatics, St. Hildegarde lived to be eighty-one, Mechthild of Magdeburg to eighty-seven, Ruysbroeck to eighty-eight, Suso to seventy, St. Teresa to sixty-seven, St. Catherine of Genoa and St. Peter of Alcantara to sixty-three. It seems as though that enhanced life which is the reward of mystical surrender enabled them to triumph over their bodily disabilities, and to live and do the work demanded of them under conditions which would have incapacitated ordinary men.

Such triumphs, which take heroic rank in the history of the human mind, have been accomplished as a rule in the same way. Like all intuitive persons, all possessors of genius, all potential artists—with whom in fact they are closely related—the mystics have, in psychological language, "thresholds of exceptional mobility." That is to say, a slight effort, a slight departure from normal conditions, will permit their latent or "subliminal" powers to emerge and occupy the mental field. A "mobile threshold" may make a man a genius, a lunatic, or a saint. All depends upon the character of the emerging powers. In the great mystic, these powers, these tracts of personality lying below the level of normal consciousness, are of unusual richness and cannot be accounted for in terms of pathology. "If it be true," says Delacroix, "that the great mystics have not wholly escaped those nervous blemishes which mark nearly all exceptional organizations, there is in them a vital and creative power, a constructive logic, an extended scale of realization—in a word, a genius—which is, in truth, their essential quality. . . . The great mystics, creators and inventors who have found a new form of life and have justified it . . . join, upon the highest summits of the human spirit, the great simplifiers of the world."

The true mystic—the person with a genius for God— hardly needs a map himself. He steers a compass course across the "vast and stormy sea of the divine." It is characteristic of his intellectual humility, however, that he is commonly willing to use the map of the community in which he finds himself, when it comes to showing other people the route which he has pursued. Sometimes these maps have been adequate. More, they have elucidated the obscure wanderings of the explorer; helped him; given him landmarks; worked out right. Time after time he puts his finger on some spot—some great hill of vision, some city of the soul—and says with conviction, "*Here* have I been." At other times the maps have embarrassed him, have refused to fit in with his description. Then he has tried, as Boehme did and after him Blake, to make new ones. Such maps are often wild in drawing, because good draftsmanship does not necessarily go with a talent for exploration. Departing from the usual convention, they are hard—sometimes impossible—to understand. As a result, the orthodox have been forced to regard their makers as madmen or heretics, when they were really only practical men struggling to disclose great matters by imperfect means.

Without prejudice to individual beliefs, and without offering an opinion as to the exclusive truth of any one religious system or revelation—for here we are concerned neither with controversy nor with apologetics—we are bound to allow as a historical fact that mysticism, so far, has found its best map in Christianity. Christian philosophy, especially that neoplatonic theology which, taking up and harmonizing all that was best in the spiritual intuitions of Greece, India, and Egypt, was developed by the great doctors of the early and mediaeval Church, supports and elucidates the revelations of the individual mystic as no other system of thought has been able to do.

We owe to the great fathers of the first five centuries— to Clement of Alexandria and Irenæus, Gregory of Nyssa and Augustine; above all to Dionysius the Areopagite, the great Christian contemporary of Proclus—the preservation of that mighty system of scaffolding which enabled the Catholic mystics to build up the towers and bulwarks of the City of God. The peculiar virtue of this Christian philosophy, that which marks its superiority to the more coldly self-consistent systems of Greece, is the fact that it re-states the truths of metaphysics in terms of personality—thus offering a third term, a "living mediator" between the Unknowable God, the unconditioned Absolute, and the conditioned self.

卐

In our study of theology we saw the Christian mystic adopting, as chart and pilot book of his voyages and adventures, the scheme of faith, and the diagram of the spiritual world, which is accepted by ordinary Christian men. We saw that he found in it a depth and richness of content which the conventional believer in that theology, the "good churchman," seldom suspects; and that which is true of the Christian mystic is also true in its measure, and as regards their respective theologies, of the Pagan, the Mohammedan, and the Buddhist.

But since the spiritual adventures of the mystic are not those of ordinary men, it will follow that this map, though always true for him, is not complete. He can press forward to countries which unmystical piety must mark as unexplored. Pushing out from harbor to "the vast and stormy sea of the divine," he can take soundings and mark dangers the existence of which such piety never needs to prove. Hence it is not strange that certain maps, artistic representations or symbolic schemes, should have come into being which describe or suggest the special experiences of the mystical consciousness, and the doctrines to which these experiences have given birth. Many of these maps have an uncouth, even an impious appearance in the eyes of those unacquainted with the facts which they attempt to translate, as the charts of the deep-sea sailor seem ugly and unintelligible things to those who have never been out of sight of land. Others—and these the most pleasing, most easily understood—have already been made familiar, perhaps tiresomely familiar, to us by the poets, who, intuitively recognizing their suggestive qualities, their links with truth, have borrowed and adapted them to their own business of translating Reality into terms of rhythm and speech. Ultimately, however, they owe their origin to the mystics, or to that mystical sense which is innate in all true poets. And in the last resort it is the mystic's kingdom, and the mystic's experience, which they affect to describe.

These special mystical diagrams, these symbolic and artistic descriptions of man's inward history—his secret adventures with God—are almost endless in their variety, since in each we have a picture of the country of the soul seen through a different temperament. To describe all would be to analyze the whole field of mystical literature, and indeed much other literature as well, to epitomize in fact all that has been dreamed and written concerning the so-called "inner life"—a dreary and lengthy task. But the majority of them, I think, express a comparatively small number of essential doctrines or fundamental ways of seeing things. And as regards their imagery, they fall into three great classes, representative of the three principal ways in which man's spiritual consciousness reacts to the touch of Reality, the three primary if paradoxical facts of which that consciousness must be aware. Hence a consideration of mystic symbols drawn from each of these groups may give us a key with which to unlock some at least of the verbal riddles of the individual adventurer.

Thanks to the spatial imagery inseparable from human thinking and human expression, no direct description of spiritual experience is or can be possible to man. It must always be symbolic, allusive, oblique, always suggest, but never tell, the truth. And in this respect there is not much to choose between the fluid and artistic language of vision and the arid technicalities of philosophy. In another respect, however, there is a great deal to choose between them, and here the visionary, not the philosopher, receives the palm. The greater the suggestive quality of the symbol used, the more answering emotion it evokes in those to whom it is addressed, the more truth it will convey. A good symbolism, therefore, will be more than mere diagram or mere allegory: it will use to the utmost the resources of beauty and of passion, will bring with it hints of mystery and wonder, and bewitch with dreamy periods the mind to which it is addressed. Its appeal will not be to the clever brain, but to the desirous heart, the intuitive sense, of man.

The three great classes of symbols which I propose to consider, appeal to three deep cravings of the self, three great expressions of man's restlessness, which only mystic truth can fully satisfy. The first is the craving which makes him a pilgrim and wanderer. It is the longing to go out from his normal world in search of a lost home, a "better country": an

Eldorado, a Sarras, a Heavenly Zion. The next is that craving of heart for heart, of the soul for its perfect mate, which makes him a lover. The third is the craving for inward purity and perfection, which makes him an ascetic, and in the last resort a saint.

These three cravings, I think, answer to three ways in which mystics of different temperaments attack the problem of the Absolute, three different formulæ under which their transcendence of the sense-world can be described. In describing this transcendence and the special adventures involved in it, they are describing a change from the state of ordinary men, in touch with the sense-world, responding to its rhythms, to the state of spiritual consciousness in which, as they say, they are "in union" with Divine Reality, with God. Whatever be the theological creed of the mystic, he never varies in declaring this close, definite, and actual intimacy to be the end of his quest. "Mark me like the tulip with Thine own streaks," says the Sufi. "I would fain be to the Eternal Goodness what his own hand is to a man," says the German contemplative. "My *me* is God, nor do I know my selfhood save in Him," says the Italian saint.

But, since this Absolute God is for him substance, ground, or underlying Reality of all that *is*—present yet absent, near yet far—He is already as truly immanent in the human soul as in the Universe. The seeker for the Real may therefore objectify his quest in two apparently contradictory, yet really mutually explanatory ways. First he may see it as an outgoing journey from the world of illusion to the real or transcendental world, a leaving of the visible for the invisible. Secondly, it may appear to him as an inward alteration, remaking or regeneration, by which his personality or character is so changed as to be able to enter into communion with that Fontal Being which he loves and desires, and is united with and dominated by the indwelling God who is the fount of his spiritual life. In the first case, the objective idea "God" is the pivot of his symbolism: the Blazing Star, or Magnet of the Universe which he has seen far off, and seeing, has worshipped and desired. In the second case, the emphasis falls on the subjective idea "Sanctity," with its accompanying consciousness of a disharmony to be abolished. The Mystic Way will then be described, not as a journey, but as an alteration of personality, the transmuting of "earthly" into "heavenly" man. Plainly these two aspects are obverse and reverse of one whole. They represent that mighty pair of opposites, Infinite and Finite, God and Self, which it is the business of mysticism to carry up into a higher synthesis. Whether the process be considered as outward search or inward change, its object and its end are the same. Man enters into that Order of Reality for which he was made, and which is indeed the inciting cause of his pilgrimage and his purification. For however great the demand on the soul's own effort may be, the initiative always lies with the living Divine World itself. Man's small desire is evoked, met, and fulfilled by the Divine Desire; his "separated will" or life becomes one with the great Life of the All.

ﭏ

This consciousness, in its various forms and degrees, is perhaps the most constant characteristic of Illumination, and makes it, for the mystic soul, a pleasure-state of the intensest kind. I do not mean by this that the subject passes months or years in a continuous ecstasy of communion with the Divine. Intermittent periods of spiritual fatigue or "aridity"—renewals of the temperamental conflicts experienced in purgation— the oncoming gloom of the Dark Night—all these may be, and often are, experienced at intervals during the Illuminated Life, as flashes of insight, indistinguishable from illumination, constantly break the monotony of the Purgative Way. But a deep certitude of the Personal Life omnipresent in the universe has been achieved; and this can never be forgotten, even though it be withdrawn. The "spirit stretching towards God" declares that it has touched Him; and its normal condition henceforth is joyous consciousness of His Presence with "many privy touchings of sweet spiritual sights and feeling, measured to us as our simpleness may bear it." Where he prefers less definite or more pantheistic language, the mystic's perceptions may take the form of "harmony with the Infinite"—the same divine music transposed to a lower key.

This "sense of God" is not a metaphor. Innumerable declarations prove it to be a consciousness as sharp as that which other men have, or think they have, of color, heat, or light. It is a well-known though usually transitory experience in the religious life, like the homing instinct of birds, a fact which can neither be denied nor explained. "How that presence is felt, it may better be known by experience than by any writing," says Hilton, "for it is the life and the love, the might and the light, the joy and the rest of a chosen soul. And therefore he that hath soothfastly once felt it he may not forbear it without pain; he may not undesire it, it is so good in itself and so comfortable. . . . He cometh privily sometimes when thou art least aware of Him, but thou shalt well know Him or He go; for wonderfully He stirreth and mightily He turneth thy heart into beholding of His goodness, and doth thine heart melt delectably as wax against the fire into softness of His love."

Modern psychologists have struggled hard to discredit this "sense of the presence," sometimes attributing it to the psychic mechanism of projection, sometimes to "wish-fulfilments" of a more unpleasant origin. The mystics, however, who discriminate so much more delicately than their critics between true and false transcendental experience, never feel any doubt about its validity. Even when their experience seems inconsistent with their theology, they refuse to be disturbed.

Thus St. Teresa writes of her own experience, with her usual simplicity and directness, "In the beginning it happened to me that I was ignorant of one thing—I did not know that God was in all things: and when He seemed to me to be so near, I thought it impossible. Not to believe that He was present was not in my power; for it seemed to me, as it were, evident that I felt there His very presence. Some unlearned men used to say to me, that He was present only by His grace. *I could not believe that,* because, as I am saying, He seemed to me to be present Himself: so I was distressed. A most learned man, of the Order of the glorious Patriarch St. Dominic, delivered me from this doubt; for he told me that He was present, and how He communed with us: this was a great comfort to me."

Again, "An interior peace, and the little strength which either pleasures or displeasures have to remove this presence (during the time it lasts) of the Three Persons, and that without power to doubt of it, continue in such a manner that I clearly seem to experience what St. John says, *That He will dwell in the soul,* and this not only by grace, but that He will also make her perceive this presence." St. Teresa's strong "immanental" bent comes out well in this passage.

Such a sense of the divine presence may go side by side with the daily life and normal mental activities of its possessor, who is not necessarily an ecstatic or an abstracted visionary, remote from the work of the world. It is true that the transcendental consciousness has now become, once for all, his center of interest; its perceptions and admonitions dominate and light up his daily life. The object of education, in the Platonic sense, has been achieved: his soul has "wheeled round from the perishing world" to "the contemplation of the real world and the brightest part thereof." But where vocation and circumstances require it, the duties of a busy outward life continue to be fulfilled with steadiness and success—and this without detriment to the soul's contemplation of the Real.

In many temperaments of the unstable or artistic type, however, this intuitional consciousness of the Absolute becomes ungovernable: it constantly breaks through, obtaining forcible possession of the mental field and expressing itself in the "psychic" phenomena of ecstasy and rapture. In others, less mobile, it wells up into an impassioned apprehension, a "flame of love" in which the self seems to "meet God in the ground of the soul." This is "pure contemplation": that state of deep supplication in which the subject seems to be "seeing, feeling, and thinking all at once." By this spontaneous exercise of all his powers under the dominion of love, the mystic attains that "Vision of the Heart" which, "more interior, perhaps, than the vision of dream or ecstasy," stretches to the full those very faculties which it seems to be holding in suspense, just as a top "sleeps" when it is spinning fast. *Ego dormio et cor meum vigilat* [I slept, but my heart was awake (Song 5:2)]. This act of contemplation, this glad surrender to an overwhelming consciousness of the Presence of God, leaves no sharp image on the mind—only a knowledge that we have been lifted up, to a veritable gazing upon That which eye hath not seen.

≽

What do these things mean for us, for the ordinary unmystical men? What are their links with that concrete world of appearance in which we are held fast, with that mysterious, ever-changing life which we are forced to lead? What do these great and strange adventures of the spirit tell us as to the goal of that lesser adventure of life on which we are set: as to our significance, our chances of freedom, our relation with the Absolute? Do they merely represent the eccentric performances of a rare psychic type? Are the matchless declarations of the contemplatives only the fruits of unbridled imaginative genius, as unrelated to reality as music to the fluctuations of the Stock Exchange? Or are they the supreme manifestation of a power which is inherent in our life: reports of observations made upon an actual plane of being, which transcends and dominates our normal world of sense? The question is vital, for unless the history of the mystics can touch and light up some part of this normal experience, take its place in the general history of man, contribute something towards our understanding of his nature and destiny, its interest for us can never be more than remote, academic, and unreal.

Far from being academic and unreal, that history, I think, is vital for the deeper understanding of the history of humanity. It shows us, upon high levels, the psychological process to which every self which desires to rise to the perception of Reality must submit, the formula under which man's spiritual consciousness, be it strong or weak, must necessarily unfold. In the great mystics we see the highest and widest development of that consciousness to which the human race has yet attained. We see its growth exhibited to us on a grand scale, perceptible of all men, the stages of its slow transcendence of the sense-world marked by episodes of splendor and of terror which are hard for common men to accept or understand as a part of the organic process of life.

But the germ of that same transcendent life, the spring of the amazing energy which enables the great mystic to rise to freedom and dominate his world, is latent in all of us, an integral part of our humanity. Where the mystic has a genius for the Absolute, we have each a little buried talent, some greater, some less. And the growth of this talent, this spark of the soul, once we permit its emergence, will conform in little ways, and according to its measure, to those laws of organic growth, these inexorable conditions of transcendence which we found to govern the Mystic Way.

Every person, then, who awakens to consciousness of a Reality which transcends the normal world of sense—however small, weak, imperfect that consciousness may be—is put upon a road which follows at low levels the path which the mystic treads at high levels. The success with which he follows this way to freedom and full life will depend on the intensity of his love and will, his capacity for self-discipline, his steadfastness and courage. It will depend on the generosity and completeness of his outgoing passion for absolute beauty, absolute goodness, or absolute truth. But if he move at all, he will move through a series of states which are, in their own small way, analogous to those experienced by the greatest contemplative on his journey towards that union with God which is the term of the spirit's ascent towards its home.

As the embryo of physical man, be he saint or savage, passes through the same stages of initial growth, so too with spiritual man. When the "new birth" takes place in him, the new life-process of his deeper self begins. The normal individual, no less than the mystic, will know that spiral ascent towards higher levels, those oscillations of consciousness between light and darkness, those odd mental disturbances, abrupt invasions from the subliminal region, and disconcerting glimpses of truth, which accompany the growth of the transcendental powers—though he may well interpret them in other than the mystic sense. He too will be impelled to drastic self-discipline, to a deliberate purging of his eyes that he may see: and, receiving a new vision of the world, he will be spurred by it to a total self-dedication, an active surrender of his whole being, to that aspect of the Infinite which he has perceived. He too will endure in little ways the psychic upheavals of the spiritual adolescence, will be forced to those sacrifices which every form of genius demands. He will know according to his measure the dreadful moments of lucid self-knowledge, the counter-balancing ecstasy of an intuition of the Real. More and more, as we study and collate all the available evidence, this fact—this law—is borne in on us: that the general movement of human consciousness, when it obeys its innate tendency to transcendence, is always the same. There is only one road from Appearance to Reality. "Men pass on, but the States are permanent for ever."

I do not care whether the consciousness be that of artist or musician, striving to catch and fix some aspect of the heavenly light or music, and denying all other aspects of the world in order to devote themselves to this, or of the humble servant of Science, purging his intellect that he may look upon her secrets with innocence of eye—whether the higher reality be perceived in the terms of religion, beauty, suffering; of human love, of goodness, or of truth. However widely these forms of transcendence may seem to differ, the mystic experience is the key to them all. All in their different ways are exhibitions here and now of the Eternal, extensions of man's consciousness which involve calls to heroic endeavor, incentives to the remaking of character about new and higher centers of life. Through each, man may rise to freedom and take his place in the great movement of the universe, may "understand by dancing that which is done." Each brings the self who receives its revelation in good faith, does not check it by self-regarding limitations, to a humble acceptance of the universal law of knowledge: the law that "we behold that which we are," and hence that "only the Real can know Reality." Awakening, Discipline, Enlightenment, Self-surrender, and Union, are the essential phases of life's response to this fundamental fact, the conditions of our attainment of Being, the necessary formulae under which alone our consciousness of any of these fringes of Eternity—any of these aspects of the Transcendent—can unfold, develop, and attain to freedom and full life.

We are, then, one and all the kindred of the mystics; and it is by dwelling upon this kinship, by interpreting—so far as we may—their great declarations in the light of our little experience, that we shall learn to understand them best. Strange and far away though they seem, they are not cut off from us by some impassable abyss. They belong to us. They are our brethren, the giants, the heroes of our race. As the achievement of genius belongs not to itself only, but also to the society that brought it forth; as theology declares that the merits of the saints avail for all; so, because of the solidarity of the human family, the supernal accomplishment of the mystics is ours also. Their attainment is the earnest-money of our eternal life. To be a mystic is simply to participate here and now in that real and eternal life, in the fullest, deepest sense which is possible to man. It is to share, as a free and conscious agent—not a servant, but a son—in the joyous travail of the Universe: its mighty onward sweep through pain and glory towards its home in God. This gift of "sonship," this power of free cooperation in the world-process, is man's greatest honor. The ordered sequence of states, the organic development, whereby his consciousness is detached from illusion and rises to the mystic freedom which conditions, instead of being conditioned by, its normal world, is the way he must tread if that sonship is to be realized. Only by this deliberate fostering of his deeper self, this transmutation of the elements of his character, can he reach those levels of consciousness upon which he hears, and responds to, the measure "whereto the worlds keep time" on their great pilgrimage towards the Father's heart. The mystic act of union, that joyous loss of the transfigured self in God, which is the crown of man's conscious ascent towards the Absolute, is the contribution of the individual to this, the destiny of the Cosmos.

The mystic knows that destiny. It is laid bare to his lucid vision, as our puzzling world of form and color is to normal sight. He is the "hidden child" of the eternal order, an initiate of the secret plan. Hence, while "all creation groaneth and travaileth," slowly moving under the spur of blind desire towards that consummation in which alone it can have rest, he runs eagerly along the pathway to reality. He is the pioneer of Life on its age-long voyage to the One, and he shows us, in his attainment, the meaning and value of that life.

This meaning, this secret plan of Creation, flames out, had we eyes to see, from every department of existence. Its exultant declarations come to us in all great music; its magic is the life of all romance. Its law—the law of love—is the substance of the beautiful, the energizing cause of the heroic. It lights the altar of every creed. All man's dreams and diagrams concerning a transcendent Perfection near him yet intangible, a transcendent vitality to which he can attain—whether he call these objects of desire God, grace, being, spirit, beauty, "pure idea"—are but translations of his deeper self's intuition of its destiny, clumsy fragmentary hints at the all-inclusive, living Absolute which that deeper self knows to be real. This supernal Thing, the adorable Substance of all that Is—the synthesis of Wisdom, Power, and Love—and man's apprehension of it, his slow remaking in its interests, his union with it at last: this is the theme of mysticism. That two-fold extension of consciousness which allows him communion with its transcendent and immanent aspects is, in all its gradual processes, the Mystic Way. It is also the crown of human evolution, the fulfillment of life, the liberation of personality from the world of appearance, its entrance into the free creative life of the Real.

Further, Christians may well remark that the psychology of Christ, as presented to us in the Gospels, is a piece with that of the mystics. In its pain and splendor, its dual character of action and fruition, it reflects their experience upon the supernal plane of more abundant life. Thanks to this fact, for them, the Ladder of Contemplation—that ladder which mediaeval thought counted as an instrument of the Passion, discerning it as essential to the true salvation of man—stretches without a break from earth to the Empyrean. It leans against the Cross; it leads to the Secret Rose. By it the ministers of Goodness, Truth, and Beauty go up and down between the transcendent and the apparent world.

Seen, then, from whatever standpoint we may choose to adopt—whether of psychology, philosophy, or religion—the adventure of the great mystics intimately concerns us. It is a master-key to man's puzzle: by its help he may explain much in his mental makeup, in his religious constructions, in his experience of life. In all these departments he perceives himself to be climbing slowly and clumsily upward toward some attainment yet unseen. The mystics, expert mountaineers, go before him and show him, if he cares to learn, the way to freedom, to reality, to peace. He cannot rise in this, his earthly existence, to the awful and solitary peak, veiled in the Cloud of Unknowing, where they meet that "death of the summit," which is declared by them to be the gate of Perfect Life. But if he choose to profit by their explorations, he may find his level, his place within the Eternal Order. He may achieve freedom, live the "independent spiritual life."

Consider once more the Mystic Way as we have traced it from its beginning. To what does it tend if not to this?

It began by the awakening within the self of a new and embryonic consciousness, a consciousness of divine reality, as opposed to the illusory sense-world in which she was immersed. Humbled, awed by the august possibilities then revealed to her, that self retreated into the "cell of self-knowledge" and there labored to adjust herself to the Eternal Order which she had perceived, stripped herself of all that opposed it, disciplined her energies, purified the organs of sense. Remade in accordance with her intuitions of reality, the "eternal hearing and seeing were revealed in her." She opened her eyes upon a world still natural, but no longer illusory, since it was perceived to be illuminated by the Uncreated Light.

She knew then the beauty, the majesty, the divinity of the living World of Becoming which holds in its meshes every living thing. She had transcended the narrow rhythm by which common men perceive but one of its many aspects, escaped the machine-made universe presented by the cinematograph of sense, and participated in the "great life of the All." Reality came forth to her, since her eyes were cleansed to see It, not from some strange far-off and spiritual country, but gently, from the very heart of things. Thus lifted to a new level, she began again her ceaseless work of growth. And because by the cleansing of the senses she had learned to see the reality which is shadowed by the sense-world, she now, by the cleansing of her will, sought to draw nearer to that Eternal Will, that Being, which life, the World of Becoming, manifests and serves. Thus, by the surrender of her selfhood in its wholeness, the perfecting of her love, she slid from Becoming to Being, and found her true life hidden in God.

Yet the course of this transcendence, this amazing inward journey, was closely linked, first and last, with the processes of human life. It sprang from that life, as man springs from the sod. We were even able to describe it under those symbolic formulae which we are accustomed to call the "laws" of the natural world. By an extension of these formulae, their logical application, we discovered a path which led us without a break from the sensible to the supra-sensible, from apparent to absolute life. There is nothing unnatural about the Absolute of the mystics: He sets the rhythm of His own universe, and conforms to the harmonies which He has made. We, deliberately seeking for that which we suppose to be spiritual, too often overlook that which alone is Real. The true mysteries of life accomplish themselves so softly, with so easy and assured a grace, so frank an acceptance of our breeding, striving, dying, and unresting world, that the unimaginative natural man—all agog for the marvelous—is hardly startled by their daily and radiant revelation of infinite wisdom and love. Yet this revelation presses incessantly upon us. Only the hard crust of surface-consciousness conceals it from our normal sight. In some least expected moment, the common activities of life in progress, that Reality in Whom the mystics dwell slips through our closed doors, and suddenly we see It at our side.

It was said of the disciples at Emmaus, *"Mensam igitur ponunt, panes cibosque offerunt, et Deum, quem in Scripturae sacrae expositione non cognoverant, in panis fractione congnoscunt"* [They sat at table and offered bread, and God, whom in the interpretation of Scriptures they did not recognize, they recognized in the breaking of the bread]. So too for us the Transcendent Life for which we crave is revealed, and our living within it, not on some remote and arid plane of being, in the cunning explanations of philosophy, but in the normal acts of our everyday experience, suddenly made significant for us. Not in the backwaters of existence, not among subtle arguments and occult doctrines, but in all those places where the direct and simple life of earth goes on. It is found in the soul of man so long as that soul is alive and growing: it is not found in any sterile place.

This fact of experience is our link with the mystics, our guarantee of the truthfulness of their statements, the supreme importance of their adventure, their closer contact with Reality. The mystics on their part are our guarantee of the end towards which the Immanent Love, the hidden steersman which dwells in our midst, is moving: our "lovely forerunners" on the path towards the Real. They come back to us from an encounter with life's most august secret, as Mary came running from the tomb; filled with amazing tidings which they can hardly tell. We, longing for some assurance, and seeing their radiant faces, urge them to pass on their revelation if they can. It is the old demand of the dim-sighted and incredulous:

"*Dic nobis Maria*
Quid vidistis in via?"

["Tell us, Mary, what did you see on the way?"] But they cannot say: we can only report fragments of the symbolic vision:

"*Angelicos testes, sudarium, et vestes*"

["Angel witnesses, the shroud, and the graveclothes"] — not the inner content, the final divine certainty. We must ourselves follow in their footsteps if we would have that.

Like the story of the Cross, so too the story of man's spirit ends in a garden—in a place of birth and fruitfulness, of beautiful and natural things. Divine Fecundity is its secret: existence, not for its own sake, but for the sake of a more abundant life. It ends with the coming forth of divine humanity, never again to leave us: living in us and with us, a pilgrim, a worker, a guest at our table, a sharer at all hazards in life. The mystics witness to this story: waking very early they have run on before us, urged by the greatness of their love. We, incapable as yet of this sublime encounter, looking in their magic mirror, listening to their stammered tidings, may see far off the consummation of the race.

According to the measure of their strength and of their passion, these, the true lovers of the Absolute, have conformed here and now to the utmost tests of divine sonship, the final demands of life. They have not shrunk from the sufferings of the cross. They have faced the darkness of the tomb. Beauty and agony alike have called them, alike have awakened a heroic response. For them the winter is over: the time of the singing of birds is come. From the deeps of the dewy garden, Life—new, unquenchable, and ever lovely—comes to meet them with the dawn.

Correspondence and Poetry

1911
From a Letter to Mrs. Heath

Please don't ever talk of "sitting at my feet" or any nonsense like that. If you knew the real animal you would be provoked to either tears or laughter at the absurdity of the idea. . . . I am not "far on" but at the very bottom.

1913

Responding to a popular demand for a presentation of her knowledge of Mysticism that would be easier to read, Evelyn Underhill prepared The Mystic Way. *She particularly wanted to communicate with readers who were outside the religious community, a difficult assignment.*

From a letter to Mrs. Heath

I'm immersed in my book, which is very difficult, but enthralling. I write all morning and read all evening, at least as long as I can, but I generally collapse with dimness of mind about nine o'clock.

The Mystic Way

From *The Mystic Way*
The first full and perfect manifestation of this life, this
peculiar psychological growth, in which human personality
in its wholeness moves to new levels and lives at a tension
hitherto unknown, establishes itself in the independent
spiritual sphere—seems to coincide with the historical
beginning of Christianity. In Jesus of Nazareth it found its
perfect thoroughfare, rose at once to its classic expression;
and the movement which He initiated, the rare human type
which He created, is in essence a genuinely biological rather
than a merely creedal or intellectual development of the
race. In it, we see life exercising her sovereign power of
spontaneous creation, breaking out on new paths.

Already, it is true, some men—peculiarly sensitive perhaps
to the first movement of life turning in a fresh direction—had
run ahead of the common experience and stumbled upon the
gateway to those paths, even taken tentative steps along the
way in which mankind was destined to be "guided and
enticed" by the indwelling Spirit of Love. They are those
whom we call "natural mystics." Their intuitions and experiences
had been variously, but always incompletely expressed: in
creed and ceremonial, in symbolic acts which suggested the
inner experience that they sought—sometimes in prophecies
understood by none but those who made them. Nor is this
inconsistent with Life's methods, as we may discern them on
other levels of activity. The *élan vital* [vital force] of the
human race is about to pour itself in a new direction. It tries

to break through, first here, next there, pressing behind the barrier of the brain. . . .

With the passing of the centuries, the conviction of this new budding and bringing forth of the "Word," the divine idea immanent in the world, grows stronger and stronger. All the prophets feel it, all agonize for it; but they do not attain to it. We watch them through the ages, ever stretching forward to something that they shall not live to see. "Like as a woman with child, that draweth near the time of her delivery, is in pain and crieth out in her pangs; so have we been before thee, O Lord. We have been with child, we have been in pain, we have as it were brought forth wind; we have not wrought any deliverance in the earth, neither have inhabitants of the world been born" (Isaiah 26:17, 18). This is the epitaph of Jewish prophecy.

Opposed, as it seems, to this line of growth, though actually representing another of life's efforts in the same direction, we have the so-called "enthusiastic religions," the mystery-cults of the antique world; dramatizing, many of them, with a certain crude intensity, that actual process of rebirth and ascent to the spiritual sphere already instinctively discerned by the spirit of life as the path upon which man's soul was destined to move. But, however close the much-advertised correspondences between the symbolic ritual of the Orphics, or of later and more elaborate mystery cults, and the interior process through which the human soul grows to conscious union with God, these sacramental dramas remain the picture of something perceived and longed for, rather than the earnest of something actually done to the participants. To "him whose initiation was recent" they may have given a vision of the Divine World: but vision alone will not quicken that "seed of the divine life . . . that has all the riches of eternity in it, and is always wanting to come to the birth in him and be alive," the seed which, once germinated, grows steadily through the seasons, nourished by the whole machinery of life, to a perfect correspondence with Reality. "Salvation and the New Birth," says Prof. Percy Gardner, "did not attain in the Pagan mysteries more than a small part, an adumbration of the meaning those phrases were to attain in developed Christianity. They only furnished the body wherein the soul was to dwell. *They only provided organs which were destined for functions as yet undeveloped.*" No doubt there were isolated spirits in whom the teaching and ritual of these mysteries really quickened the "spark of the soul," initiated a life-movement; as there were others who rose, like St. Augustine, through the sublime speculations of Greek philosophy to a brief intellectual vision of That Which Is. But evidence of this spiritual precocity is lost to us. We find ample record of the craving, little of the attainment. The Græco-Roman world, which has bequeathed to us the rich results of its genius for beauty and for abstract thought, even for ethics of the loftiest kind, and the life-history of its many heroic men of action gives us no work either of pure literature or of biography in which we can recognize—as we may in so many records of the Mohammedan as well as the Christian world—the presence of that peculiar spiritual genius which we call "sanctity."

While no reasonable student of mysticism would wish to deny the debt which our spiritual culture owes to Greek thought, it remains true that the gift of Hellenism here has often been misconstrued. Hellenism gave to the spirit of man, not an experience, but a reading of experience. In the mysteries, the natural mystic saw a drama of his soul's adventures upon the quest of God. In Neoplatonism he founded a philosophic explanation of his most invincible desires, his most sublime perceptions: "saw from a wooded height the land of peace, but not the road thereto." Greece taught first the innately mystical, and afterwards the typically

Christian soul, how to understand itself; it produced the commentary, but not the text. Paul, caught up to the third heaven, had little to learn from the Platonic ecstasy; and it was not from Dionysus or Cybele that the mystic of the Fourth Gospel learned the actual nature of New Birth.

The "mysteries," in fact, were essentially magical dramas which stimulated the latent spiritual faculties of man, sometimes in a noble, but sometimes also in an ignoble way. Their initiates were shown the symbols of that consummation which they longed for, the union with God which is the object of all mysticism. They passed, by submission to ceremonial obligations, through stages which curiously anticipated the actual processes of life; sometimes, as in the primitive rites of the Dionysus cult, induced in themselves an artificial state of ecstasy by the use of dancing, music, and perfumes. Antiquity shows us everywhere these dramas, always built more or less according to the same pattern, because always trying to respond to the same need—the craving of the crescent soul for purity, liberation, reality, and peace. But the focal point in them was always the obtaining of personal safety or knowledge by the performance of special and sacred acts: at the utmost, by a temporary change of consciousness deliberately induced, as in ecstasy. They implied the existence of a static, ready-made spiritual world, into which the initiate could be inserted by appropriate disciplines, thereby escaping from the tyranny and unreality of the Here-and-Now. Far from being absorbed into the Christian movement, they continued side by side with it. The true descendants of the Pagan *mystes* are not the Christian mystics, as certain modern scholars would pretend; these have little in common with them but an unfortunate confusion of name. Their posterity is rather to be sought among that undying family of more or less secret associations which perpetuated this old drama of regeneration, and insisted on attributing to its merely ritual performance an awful significance, a genuine value for life. In early times the Manichæans and the Gnostics, with their elaborate but confused systems of mixed Pagan and Christian ideas, later the Rosicrucians, the Cabalists, the Freemasons, and later still the Martinists and other existing societies of "initiates," which lay claim to the possession of jealously guarded secrets of a spiritual kind, have continued the effort to find a "way out" along this road: but in vain. Not a new creation, but at best a protective mimicry, is all that life can manage here.

More and more as we proceed, the peculiar originality of the true Christian mystic becomes clear to us. We are led towards the conclusion—a conclusion which rests on historical rather than religious grounds—that the first person to exhibit in their wholeness the spiritual possibilities of man was the historic Christ; and to the corollary, that the great family of the Christian mystics—that is to say, all those individuals in whom an equivalent life-process is set going and an equivalent growth takes place—represents to us the substance of things hoped for, the evidence of things not seen, in respect of the upward movement of the racial consciousness. This family constitutes a true variation of the human species—in Leuba's words, "one of the most amazing and profound variations which have yet been witnessed"—producing, as it seems to other men, a "strange and extravagant" and yet a "heroic" type. There is in them, says Delacroix, "a vital and creative power"; they "have found a new form of life, and have justified it."

This new form of life, as it is lived by the members of this species, the peculiar psychic changes to which they must all submit, whatsoever the historic religion to which they belong, may reasonably be called Christian, since its classic expression is seen only in the Founder of Christianity. But this is not to limit it to those who have accepted the theological system called by His name. "There is," says Law, "but one salvation for all mankind, and that is the Life of God in the soul. God has but one design or intent towards all Mankind, and that is to introduce or generate His own Life, Light, and Spirit in them. . . . There is but one possible way for Man to attain this salvation, or Life of God in the soul. There is not one for the Jew, another for a Christian, and a third for the Heathen. No; God is one, human nature is one, salvation is one, and the way to it is one." We may, then, define the Christian life and the Christian growth as a movement towards the attainment of this Life of Reality, this spiritual consciousness. It is a phase of the cosmic struggle of spirit with recalcitrant matter, of mind with the conditions that hem it in. More abundant life, said the great mystic of the Fourth Gospel, is its goal; and it sums up and makes effective all the isolated struggles towards such life and such liberty which earlier ages had produced.

Christianity, of course, has often been described as a "life." The early Christians themselves called it not a belief, but a "way"—a significant fact, which the Church too quickly forgot; and the realist who wrote the Fourth Gospel called its Founder both *the* life and *the* way. But these terms have been employed by all later theologians with a discreet vagueness, have been accepted in an artistic rather than a scientific sense, with the result that Christianity as a life has meant almost anything, from obedience to a moral or even an ecclesiastical code at one end of the scale, to the enjoyment of peculiar spiritual sensations at the other. I propose, then, to define and demonstrate as clearly as I can, by the help of the only possible authorities—those who have lived it—what is really meant by the phrase "Christianity is a life." Nor is this done by way of apologetic, but rather by way of exploration. History and psychology will be our primary interests; and should theological conclusions emerge, this will be by accident rather than design.

The beginning of Christianity, we say, seems to represent the first definite emergence of a new kind of life; at first— yes, and still, for nineteen hundred years are little in the deep and steady flow of so mighty a process of becoming—a small beginning. Very, very slowly, the new type of human consciousness emerged. Here one, and there another possessed it: the thin bright chain of the Christian mystics stretching across the centuries. We see clearly, when we have cleansed our vision of obscuring prejudices, that Jesus, from the moment of His attainment of full spiritual self-consciousness, was aware that life must act thus. Loisy is doubtless right in stating that He "intended to found no religion." In His own person He was lifting humanity to new levels; giving in the most actual and concrete sense new life, a new direction of movement, to "the world"—the world for man being, of course, no more and no less than the total content of his consciousness. The "revelation" then made was not merely moral or religious: it was in the strictest sense biological. "We may assume," says Harnack most justly, "what position we will in regard to Him and His message; certain it is that thence onward the value of our race is enhanced."

But such a gift can only gradually be disclosed, only gradually be appropriated. Those who can appropriate, who can move in this fresh direction, grow to this state of high tension, develop this spiritual consciousness—these are the "little flock" to whom the Kingdom, the Realm of Reality, is given. These, not the strenuous altruist nor the orthodox believer, are the few chosen out of the many called: actual centers of creative life, agents of divine fecundity, the light, the salt, the leaven, the pathfinders of the race. It is the glory of Christianity that, hidden though they be by the more obvious qualities of the superstitious and the ecclesiastically minded, these vital souls have never failed the Church. Thus "by personal channels—the flame of the human and

humanizing Spirit passing from soul to soul—there has come
down to our days, along with a great mass of nominal or
corrupt Christianity, a true and lineal offspring of the Church
established on the Rock."

It is true that mystical Christianity offers infinitely
graded possibilities of attainment to the infinitely graded
variations of human temperament, love, and will. But all
these graded paths take a parallel course. All run, as Dante
saw, towards the concentric circles of the same heaven, a
heaven which has many mansions, but all built upon the
same plan. It deals, from first to last, with the clear and
victorious emergence of the spiritual in the Here-and-
Now, and with the balanced response of the total spirit of
man to that declared Reality. Its history purports to tell
us how this revelation and response happened once for all
in a complete and perfect sense, how the Divine Life nesting
within the world broke through and expressed itself,
thereby revealing new directions along which human life
could cut its way. Its psychology tries to describe how life
has attacked those new paths, the phenomena which
attend on and express the evolution of the Christian soul,
the state of equilibrium to which that soul attains. It
demonstrates over and over again that the little company
of its adepts—and those other born lovers of reality who
went with them "not knowing what they sought"—have all
passed by the same landmarks and endured the same
adventures in the course of their quest. In all, the same
essential process—the steadfast loving attention to some
aspect of Transcendent Reality perceived, and the active
movement of response—has led to the same result: growth
towards new levels, transmutation of character, closer and
closer identification with the Divine Life. In every such
case the individual has learned "to transfer himself from a
center of self-activity into an organ of revelation of universal

being, to live a life of affection for, and oneness with, the larger life outside."

The proposition that this quest and this achievement constitute an egotistical and "world renouncing religion" suited only to contemplatives, is only less ridiculous than the more fashionable delusion which makes Christianity the religion of social amiability, democratic ideals, and "practical common sense." On the contrary, the true mystic quest may as well be fulfilled in the market as in the cloister, by Joan of Arc on the battlefield as by Simeon Stylites on his pillar. It is true that since human vitality and human will are finite, many of the great mystics have found it necessary to concentrate their love and their attention on this one supreme aspect of the "will-to-live." Hence the cloistered mystic and the recluse obeys a necessity of his own nature, the necessity which has produced specialists in every art. But the life for which he strives if he achieves it, floods the totality of his being: the "energetic" no less than the "contemplative" powers. It regenerates, enriches, lifts to new heights of vision, will, and love, the whole man, not some isolated spiritual part of him, and sends him back to give, according to his action, "more abundant life" to the surrounding world. The real achievements of Christian mysticism are more clearly seen in Catherine of Siena regenerating her native city, Joan of Arc leading the armies of France, Ignatius creating the Society of Jesus, Fox giving life to the Society of Friends, than in all the ecstasies and austerities of the Egyptian "fathers in the desert." That mysticism is an exhibition of the higher powers of love, a love which would face all obstacles, endure all purifications, and cherish and strive for the whole world. In all its variations, it demands one quality—humble and heroic effort; and it points with a steady finger to one road from Appearance to Reality—the Mystic Way, Transcendence.

As in those who pass through the normal stages of bodily and mental development, so in those who tread this Mystic Way—though the outward circumstances of their lives may differ widely—we always see the same thing happening, the same sort of growth taking place.

The American psychologist Dr. Stanley Hall has pointed out that as the human embryo was said by the earlier evolutionists to recapitulate in the course of its development the history of ascending life, to the point at which it touches humanity—presenting us, as it were, month by month, with plastic sketches of the types by which it had passed—so the child and youth do really continue that history, exhibiting stage by stage dim and shadowy pictures of the progress of humanity itself.

Thus the vigorous period of childhood from eight to twelve years of age, with its practical outdoor interests and instinct for adventure, represents a distinct stage in human evolution: the making of "primitive" man, a strong, intelligent animal, utterly individualistic, wholly concentrated on the will-to-live. In the formation of the next type, which is the work of the adolescent period, we see reproduced before us one of nature's "fresh starts": the spontaneous development of a new species, by no means logically deducible from the well-adapted animal which preceded it. Much that characterized the child-species is now destroyed; new qualities develop amid psychic and physical disturbance, "a new wave of vitality" lifts the individual to fresh levels, a veritable "new birth" takes place.

Normal human adolescence is thus "an age of all-sided and saltatory development, when new traits, powers, faculties, and dimensions, which have no other nascent period, arise." It is not merely deduced from the childhood which preceded it: it is one of life's creative epochs, when the creature finds itself re-endowed with energy of a new and higher type, and the Ego acquires a fresh center. "In some respects early adolescence is thus the infancy of man's higher nature, when he receives from the great all-mother his last capital of energy and evolutionary momentum." "Psychic adolescence," says this same authority, "is heralded by all-sided mobilization." As the child, so again the normal adult; each represents a terminal stage of human development. Each is well adjusted to his habitual environment; and were adaptation to such environment indeed the "object" of the life-spirit, the experience of "the boy who never grew up" might well be the experience of the race.

But ascending life cannot rest in old victories. "At dawning adolescence this old unity and harmony with nature is broken up; the child is driven from his paradise and must enter upon a long viaticum of ascent, must conquer a higher kingdom of man for himself, break out a new sphere and evolve a more modern story to his psycho-physical nature. Because his environment is to be far more complex, the combinations are less stable, the ascent less easy and secure. . . . New dangers threaten on all sides. It is the most critical stage of life, because failure to mount almost always means retrogression, degeneracy, or fall."

In the making of spiritual man, that "new creature," we seem to see this process again repeated. He is the "third race" of humanity, as the Romans, with their instinct for realism, called in fact the Christian type when first it arose among them. Another wave of vitality now rolls up from the deeps with its "dower of energy"; another stage in life's ascent is attacked. Mind goes back into the melting pot, that fresh powers and faculties may be born. The true mystic, indeed, is the adolescent of the infinite; for he looks forward during the greater part of his career—that long upward climb towards a higher kingdom—to a future condition of maturity. From first to last he exhibits all the characteristics of youth; he never loses—as that arrested thing, the normal adult must—the freshness of his reactions on the world. He has the spontaneity, the responsiveness, the instability of youth; he experiences all its struggles and astonishments. He is swept by exalted feeling, is capable of ideal vision and quixotic adventure: there is "color in his soul."

As with the adolescent of the physical order, the mystic's entrance on this state, this new life—however long and carefully prepared by the steady pressure of that transcendent side of nature we call "grace," and by his own interior tendency of "love"—yet seems when it happens to be cataclysmic and abrupt: abrupt as birth, since it always means the induction of consciousness into an order previously unknown. The *élan vital* is oriented in a new direction and begins the hard work of cutting a fresh path. At once, with its first movement, new levels of reality are disclosed, a transformation both in the object and in the intensity of feeling takes place. The self moves in both an inner and an outer "world unrealized."

As the self-expression of the Divine Life in the world conforms to a rhythm too great for us to grasp, so that its manifestation appears to us erratic and unprepared, so is it with the self-expression, the emergence into the field of consciousness, of that fontal life of man which we have called the soul's spark or seed, which takes place in the spiritual adolescence. This emergence is seldom understood by the self in relation with life as a whole. It seems to him a separate gift or "grace," infused from without, rather than developed from within. It startles him by its suddenness, by the gladness, awe, and exaltation which it brings: an emotional inflorescence, parallel with that which announces the birth of perfect human love. This moment is the spiritual springtime. It comes, like the winds of March, full of natural wonder; and gives to all who experience it a participation in the deathless magic of eternal springs. An enhanced vitality, a wonderful sense of power and joyful apprehension as towards worlds before ignored or unknown, floods the consciousness. Life is raised to a higher degree of tension than ever before; and therefore to a higher perception of Reality.

> O glory of the lighted mind,
> How dead I'd been, how dumb, how blind.
> The station brook, to my new eyes,
> Was babbling out of Paradise,
> The waters rushing from the rain
> Where singing Christ has risen again.
> I thought all earthly creatures knelt
> From rapture of the joy I felt.
> The narrow station-wall's brick ledge,
> The wild hop withering in the hedge,
> The lights in huntsman's upper story,
> Were parts of an eternal glory,
> Were God's eternal garden flowers.
> I stood in bliss at this for hours.
>   John Masefield, *The Everlasting Mercy*

The exaltation of Saul Kane, the converted poacher, here breaks into an expression which could be paralleled by many a saint. By the unknown poet of the "Odes of Solomon" crying, "Everything became like a relic of Thyself, and a memorial for ever of Thy faithful works." By Angela of Foligno, to whom, as she climbed the narrow pathway from the vale of Spello to Assisi, and looked at the vineyards on either hand, the Holy Spirit perpetually said, "Look and see! This is My Creation"; so that suddenly the sight of these natural things filled her with ineffable delight. By St. Teresa, who was much helped in the beginning of her spiritual life by looking at fields, water, and flowers; for "In them I saw traces of the Creator—I mean that the sight of these things was as a book unto me." By George Fox, to whom at the time of his first mystic illuminations, "all creation gave another smell beyond what words can utter." By Brother Lawrence receiving from the leafless tree "a high view of the providence and power of God." By the Sufi, for whom "when the mystery of the essence of being has been revealed to him, the furnace of the world becomes transformed into a garden of flowers," so that "the adept sees the almond through the envelope of its shell; and, no longer beholding himself, perceives only his Friend; in all that he sees, beholding his face, in every atom perceiving the whole."

All these have experienced all abrupt access of divine vitality: rolling up they know not whence, breaking old barriers, overflowing the limits of old conceptions, changing their rhythm of receptivity, the quality of their attention to life. They are regenerate, entinctured and fertilized by somewhat not themselves. Hence, together with this new power pouring in on them, they receive new messages of wonder and beauty from the external world. New born, they stand here at the threshold of illimitable experiences, in which life's powers of ecstasy and of endurance, of love and of pain, shall be exploited to the full.

This change of consciousness, this conversion, most often happens at one of two periods: at the height of normal adolescence, about eighteen years of age, before the crystallizing action of maturity has begun; or, in the case of those finer spirits who have carried into manhood the adolescent faculties of growth and response, at the attainment of full maturity, about thirty years of age. It may, however, happen at any time; for it is but an expression of that life which is "movement itself." During epochs of great mystical activity, such as that which marked the "apostolic age" of Christianity, the diffused impulse to transcendence—a veritable "wind of the spirit"—stimulates to new life all whom it finds in its way. The ordinary laws of growth are then suspended, and minds

in every stage of development are invaded by the flooding
tide of the spiritual consciousness.

The stages of growth which follow are well known to
mystical and ascetic literature. Here conditions of stress and
of attainment, each so acutely felt as to constitute states of
pain and of pleasure, alternate with one another—sometimes
rapidly, sometimes in long, slow rhythms—until the new life
aimed at is at last established and a state of equilibrium
assured. First after the joy of "rebirth" there comes a period of
difficult growth and effort, the hard and painful readjustment
to a new order, the disciplines and renunciations in which the
developing soul remakes its inner world. All that helps life to
move in the new direction must now be established. The
angle of the mental blinkers must be altered, attention
focused on the new outlook. All that holds the self back to a
racial past, the allurements of which have now become a
retarding influence or "sin," must be renounced.

This process, in its countless forms, is Purgation. Here it
is inevitable that there should be much struggle, difficulty,
actual pain. Man, hampered by strong powers and instincts
well adapted to the life he is leaving, is candidate for a new
and higher career to which he is not fully adapted yet. Hence
the need for that asceticism, the training of the athlete,
which every race and creed has adopted as the necessary
preliminary of the mystic life. The period of transition, the
rearrangement of life, must include something equivalent to
the irksome discipline of the schoolroom, to the deliberate
curbing of wild instincts long enjoyed. It is, in fact, a period
of education, of leading forth, in which much that gave zest
to his old life is taken away, and much that is necessary to the
new life is poured upon him through his opening faculties,
though in a form which he cannot yet enjoy or understand.

Next, the period of education completed, and those new
powers or virtues which are the "ornaments of the spiritual

marriage" put on, the trained and purified consciousness emerges into that clear view of the Reality in which it lives and moves, which is known sometimes as the "practice of the Presence of God," or, more generally, as *Illumination.* "Grace," the transcendent life force, surges up ever stronger from the deeps—"wells up within, like a fountain of the Spirit"— forming new habits of attention and response in respect of the supernal world. The faculty of contemplation may now develop, new powers are born, the passion of love is disciplined and enhanced.

Though this stage of growth is called by the old writers on mysticism "the state proper to those that be in progress," it seems in the completeness of its adaptation to environment to mark a "terminal point" of spiritual development—one of the halts in the upward march of the soul—and does, in fact, mark it for many an individual life, which never moves beyond this level of reality. Yet, it is no blind alley, but lies upon the highway of life's ascent to God. In the symbolic language of the Sufis, it is the Tavem, where the pilgrim rests and is refreshed by "the draught of Divine Love," storing up the momentum necessary for the next "saltatory development" of life.

True to that strange principle of oscillation and instability, keeping the growing consciousness swinging between states of pleasure and states of pain—which seems, so far as our perception goes, to govern the mystery of growth—this development, when it comes, destroys the state which pre- ceded it as completely as the ending of childhood destroys the harmonious universe of the child. Strange cravings which it cannot understand now invade the growing self: the languor and gloom, the upheavals and loss of equilibrium, which adolescents know so well. Like the young of civilized man, here spiritual man is "reduced back to a state of nature, so far as some of the highest faculties are concerned, again helpless, in need not only of guidance, but of shelter and protection. His knowledge of self is less adequate, and he must slowly work out his salvation." This is the period of spiritual confusion and impotence, the last drastic purification of the whole character, the remaking of personality in accordance with the demands of the transcendent sphere, which is called by some mystics the *Dark Night of the Soul,* by others the "spiritual death," or "purgation of the will." Whatever the psychological causes which produce it, all mystics agree that this state constitutes a supreme moral crisis, in which the soul is finally cleansed of all attachments to self-hood, and is utterly surrendered to the purposes of the Divine Life. Spiritual man is driven from his old paradise, enters on a new period of struggle, must evolve "another story to his soul."

The result of this pain and effort is the introduction of the transmuted self into that state of Union, or complete harmony with the divine, towards which it had tended from the first: a state of equilibrium, of enhanced vitality and freedom, in which the spirit is at last full-grown and capable of performing the supreme function of maturity—giving birth to new spiritual life. Here man indeed receives his last and greatest "dower of vitality and momentum"; for he is now an inheritor of the Universal Life, a "partaker of the Divine Nature." "My life shall be a real life, being wholly full of Thee."

> Mankind, like water fowl, are sprung from the sea—
>   the sea of the soul;
> Risen from that sea, why should the bird make here his home?
> Nay, we are pearls in that sea, therein we all abide;
> Else, why does wave follow wave from the sea of soul?
> 'Tis the time of union's attainment, 'tis the time of eternity's
>   beauty,
> 'Tis the time of favor and largesse, 'tis the ocean of perfect purity.

The billow of largesse hath appeared, the thunder of the sea
  hath arrived,
The morn of blessedness hath dawned. Morn? No, 'tis the light
  of God.
  —Jalalu'ddin, *Divan*

Now it is exactly this growth in vitality, this appropriation of the "billow of largesse"—called by her theologians "prevenient grace"—which Christianity holds out as the ideal not merely of the religious aristocrat, but of all mankind. It is a growth which goes the whole way from "earth" to "heaven," from the human to the divine, and may as easily be demonstrated by the processes of psychology as by the doctrines of religion. At once "natural" and "supernatural," it tends as much to the kind of energy called active as to the other, rarer kind of energy called contemplative. "Primarily a life of pure inwardness, its conquests are in the invisible; but since it represents the life of the All, so far as man is able to attain that Life, it must show results in the All." Its end is the attainment of that "kingdom" which it is the one business of Christianity to proclaim. She enshrined the story of this growth in her liturgy, she has always demanded it in its intensest form from all her saints, she trains to it every novice in her religious orders—more, every Christian in the world to whom his faith means more than assent to a series of creedal definitions. As we shall see, when she asks the neophyte to "imitate Christ" she is implicitly asking him to set in hand this organic process of growth. Whether the resultant character tends most to contemplation or to action will depend upon individual temperament. In either case it will be a character of the mystical type; for its reaction upon life will be conditioned by the fact that it is a partaker of Reality.

If the theory which is here outlined be accepted, it will follow that Christianity cannot be understood apart from the psychological process which it induces in those who receive it in its fullness. Hence the only interpreters of Christian doctrine to whose judgment we are bound to submit will be those in whom this process of development has taken place, who are proved to have followed "the Mystic Way," attained that consciousness, that independent spiritual life, which alone is really Christian, and therefore know the realities of which they speak. Thus not only St. Paul and the writer of the Fourth Gospel, but also St. Macarius or St. Augustine will become for us "inspired" in this sense. So too will later interpreters, later exhibitors of this new direction of life: the great mystics of the mediæval period. Those who lived the life outside the fold will also help us—Plotinus, the Sufis, Blake. "My teaching is not mine, but His that sent me: if any man willeth to do His will, *he* shall know of the teaching."

"Just as we cannot obtain," says Harnack, "a complete knowledge of a tree without regarding not only its root and its stem, but also its bark, its branches, and the way in which it blooms, so we cannot form any right estimate of the Christian religion unless we take our stand upon a comprehensive induction that shall cover all the facts of its history. It is true that Christianity has had its classical epoch; nay more, it had a Founder who Himself was what He taught—to steep ourselves in Him is still the chief matter; but to restrict ourselves to Him means to take a point of view too low for His significance. . . . He had his eye on *man*, in whatever external situation he might be found—upon *man*, who fundamentally always remains the same." Man, the thoroughfare of Life upon her upward pilgrimage; self-creative, susceptible of freedom, able to breathe the atmosphere of Reality, to attain consciousness here and now of the Spiritual World.

applied spirituality

1915-1924

Practical Mysticism

1915

The majority of Evelyn Underhill's books are relatively slim volumes. One of those little books, Practical Mysticism, *is another attempt to reach the religious interests of those who are not actively involved with organized religion. Even so, a Bishop commented, "I had been prepared for its message by many years of searching without finding, and it spoke straight to the heart of my condition. . . . It is the book to which I owe more than to any other theological book I have ever had."*

From *Practical Mysticism*

Those who are interested in that special attitude towards the universe which is now loosely called "mystical," find themselves beset by a multitude of persons who are constantly asking—some with real fervor, some with curiosity, and some with disdain—"What is mysticism?" When referred to the writings of the mystics themselves, and to other works in which this question appears to be answered, these people reply that such books are wholly incomprehensible to them.

On the other hand, the genuine inquirer will find before long a number of self-appointed apostles who are eager to answer his question in many strange and inconsistent ways, calculated to increase rather than resolve the obscurity of his mind. He will learn that mysticism is a philosophy, an illusion, a kind of religion, a disease; that it means having visions, performing conjuring tricks, leading an idle, dreamy, and selfish life, neglecting one's business, wallowing in vague spiritual emotions, and being in tune with the infinite. He

will discover that it emancipates him from all dogmas—
sometimes from all morality—and at the same time that it is
very superstitious. One expert tells him that it is simply
"Catholic piety," another that Walt Whitman was a typical
mystic; a third assures him that all mysticism comes from the
East, and supports his statement by an appeal to the mango
trick.* At the end of a prolonged series of lectures, sermons,
tea-parties, and talks with earnest persons, the inquirer is still
heard saying too often in tones of exasperation—"What *is*
mysticism?"

I dare not pretend to solve a problem which has provided
so much good hunting in the past. It is indeed the object of
this little essay to persuade the practical man to the one
satisfactory course: that of discovering the answer for
himself. Yet perhaps it will give confidence if I confess at the
outset that I have discovered a definition which to me
appears to cover all the ground; or at least, all that part of the
ground which is worth covering. It will hardly stretch to the
mango trick; but it finds room at once for the visionaries and
philosophers, for Walt Whitman and the saints.

Here is the definition:

Mysticism is the art of union with Reality. The mystic is
a person who has attained that union in greater or less
degree, or who aims at and believes in such attainment.

It is not expected that the inquirer will find great comfort
in this sentence when it first meets his eye. The ultimate
question, "What is Reality?"—a question, perhaps, which
never occurred to him before—is already forming in his
mind; and he knows it will cause him infinite distress. Only a
mystic can answer it: and he, in terms which other mystics
alone will understand. Therefore, for the time being, the
practical man may put it on one side. All that he is asked to
consider now is this: that the word "union" represents not so
much a rare and unimaginable operation, as something which

he is dong, in a vague, imperfect fashion, at every moment of his conscious life—and doing with intensity and thoroughness in all the more valid moments of that life. We know a thing only by uniting with it, by assimilating it, by an interpenetration of it and ourselves. It gives itself to us, just in so far as we give ourselves to it; and it is because our outflow towards things is always so perfunctory and so languid, that our comprehension of things is so perfunctory and languid too. The great Sufi who said, "Pilgrimage to the place of the wise, is to escape the flame of separation," spoke the literal truth. Wisdom is the fruit of communion; ignorance is the inevitable portion of those who "keep themselves to themselves," and stand apart, judging, analyzing the things which they have never truly known.

Poetry

1908

MISSA CANTATA
Once in an abbey-church, the while we prayed,
    All silent at the lifting of the Host,
A little bird through some high window strayed;
        And to and fro
      Like a wee angel lost
That on a sudden finds its heaven below,
      It went the morning long
And made our Eucharist more glad with song.

It sang, it sang! And as the quiet priest
    Far off about the lighted altar moved,
The awful substance of the mystic feast
        All hushed before
      It like a thing that loved,
Yet loved in liberty, would plunge and soar
      Beneath the vault in play
And thence toss down the oblation of its lay.

The walls that went our sanctuary around
    Did as of old, to that sweet summons yield.
New scents and sounds within our gates were found,
        The cry of kine,
      The fragrance of the field,
All woodland whispers, hastened to the shrine,
      The country side was come
Eager and joyful, to its spirit's home.

Far stretched I saw the cornfield and the plough,
    The scudding cloud, the cleanly running brook,
The humble kindly turf, the tossing bough,
        That all their light
        From Love's own furnace took;
This altar, where one angel brownly bright

    Proclaimed the sylvan creed,
And sang the Benedictus of the mead.

All earth was lifted to communion then,
    All lovely life was there to meet its King;
Ah, not the little arid souls of men
        But sun and wind
        And all desirous thing
The ground of their beseeching here did find;
        All with one self same bread,
And all by one eternal priest were fed.

CONTINUOUS VOYAGE

At twilight, when I lean the gunwale o'er
And watch the water turning from the bow,
I sometimes think the best is here and now—
The voyage all, and naught the hidden shore.
Is there no help? And must we make the land?
Shall every sailing in some haven cease?
And must the chain rush out, the anchor strike the sand,
And is there from its fetters no release?
And shall the steersman's voice say, "Nevermore
The ravening gale, the soft and sullen fog,
No more the cunning shoal, the changeful ebb and flow.
Put up the charts, and take the lead below,
And close the vessel's log"?

Adventure is a seaman's life, the port
Calls but the weary, and the tempest driven:
Perhaps its safety were too dearly bought
If that for this our freedom must be given.
For lo! Our Steersman is forever young
And with much gladness sails beneath the stars;
Our ship is old, yet still her sails are hung
Like eager wings upon the steady spars.
Then tell me not of havens for the soul
Where tides can never come, nor storms molest;
My sailing spirit seeks no sheltered goal,
Naught is more sad than safety—life is best
When every day brings danger for delight,
And each new solemn night
Engulfs our whitening wake within the whole.

Beyond the bent horizon oceans are
Where every star
Lies like an isle upon Eternity.
There would I be
Given to his rushing wind,
No prudent course to find
For some snug corner of Infinity;
But evermore to sail
Close reefed before the gale,
And see the steep
Great billow of his love, with threatening foam
Come roaring home
And lift my counter in its mighty sweep.

Addresses and Articles

1922

Many of the most revealing insights into Evelyn Underhill's spiritual development may be gleaned from the articles and talks she prepared for various clubs and organizations. Three examples follow.

From the address to the Guild of Health Here we are, little half-animal, half-spiritual creatures, mysteriously urged from within, and enticed from without to communion with spiritual Reality. If and when we surrender to this craving and this attraction, we enter thereby—though at first dimly—on a completely new life full of variety, of new joy, tension, and pain, offering an infinite opportunity of development to us. Such is the life of prayer as understood by the mystics, and as practiced with greater or less completeness of surrender and reward by all real lovers of Christ. . . . We take as our first principle the humble and diligent use of the degree of prayer natural to a soul at any particular stage of its course, and not the anxious straining towards some other degree yet beyond it.

1922

From the Swanwick Conference, July, 1922 It is the double simultaneous outstretching that matters; this only can open the heart wide enough to let in God, and so make each man who achieves it a mediator of His Reality to other men. The non-religious socialist seems to stretch out one hand, and the non-social pietist the other. But one without the other is useless. Both at once: that is where the difficulty comes in.

It sometimes seems a demand which we can hardly meet.

1923

From *Girls' Club News*, January 23, 1923
However ardent the spiritual or idealistic inclinations of the club leader or worker may be, these inclinations should not be too prominent in her behavior and must *never* be taken as a standard to which others are to be deliberately tuned up. They make their best effect casually and without observation. Keep the home fires burning by all means; they are the fires which raise the steam by which you do your work. But don't keep poking them in public and remarking on the quality of the coal. The gentle glow they spread is their best recommendation. . . .

Be sure that religion is never offered to the young as primarily something which will be a comfort to them, or out of which they can get something for themselves. . . . Generosity of outlook is one of the qualities most needed for a healthy spiritual life.

Personal Journal and Correspondence

Most revealing of all are the unguarded notes Evelyn Underhill made to herself. The "Green Notebook" was kept during 1923 and 1924. The "Green and Flowered Notebooks" were written during the period that stretched from 1926 to 1937. These private records of her spiritual journey are startling, in that her public presence did not betray the depth of her struggles. They are also reassuring to many of us who experience similar tensions.

FEBRUARY, 1923

Such lights as one gets are now different in type: less overwhelming in their emotional result: quite independent of "sensible devotion." More quiet, calm, expansive, like intellectual intuitions yet not quite that either. Thus yesterday I *saw* and felt *how* it actually is, that we are in Christ and He in us—the interpenetration of Spirit—and all of us merged together in Him actually, and so justly described as His body. The way to full intercessory power must, I think, be along this path. Quite half of what I saw slipped away from me, but the certitude remains: "the fragrance of those desirable meats," as St. Augustine says. Curious how keen all the Saints are about food. . . .

More and more I should like to get away from sensible consolations or at least their dominance. They are entrancing and overwhelming; but they don't really lead anywhere. It's the deep, quiet, mysterious love one wants to keep, and gradually transfer focus to the *will*. Sink down and down just grateful to be there—an almost invisible speck in the ocean, so the degree of blackness doesn't matter much. Vivid experiences are not over after all, as I fancied. But I don't really want them any more. Not perfectly sure they are pure and beyond suspicion. My own feeling state enters in too much: the other is not mine at all but an edgeless, penetrating love and joy—"the love wherewith the heart loves Thee."

MARCH 16, 1923

Been through a black bit lately—over mastering suggestion that after all, my whole invisible experience *was* only subjective. There's *no* test—nothing to lay hold of—I might right through have been deceived. Once this lodges in one's mind it's absolutely paralyzing. All the books say these things in unmortified beginners are "very suspicious"—so, what *can* one think? So easy to suggest to one's self—always reading these things—and yet the reality doesn't match the books. One *couldn't* deduce it from them—and it's on levels infinitely beyond me. The only thing is to ask the Baron and accept his judgment as *final*.

After it was over—but only set aside, not solved—swing back to a divine inner peace, sometimes like a continuous music but not distracting—just joy. Getting easier now to make instantaneous refusals of pleasures, etc., and dismiss them as soon as renounced—as if one were being backed up, and *more* each time one makes oneself do this. It's a more and *more* mysterious life. I'm still far too critical, too dogmatic, fond of my own view, not *nearly* gentle and humble enough in giving advice.

FEBRUARY 13, 1923

For a moment, I saw the "Universe that thinks and knows."
This solves all Christological problems in a flash. I suppose
that *sort* of knowledge is what is meant by "spiritual truths
spiritually discerned."

FEBRUARY 18, 1923

This morning, not well enough to go to Communion.
Stayed in bed: worried by feeling perhaps I was *really* well
enough to risk it. Read Sunday prayers. Always fancied I
couldn't *really* pray in bed—must kneel on a hard floor.
When I'd finished, turned to God in prayer; and suddenly
the Spirit of Christ came right into my soul—as it were,
transfusing it in every part. How could I imagine this? I
wasn't excited, but deeply happy and awed. So intimate,
all-penetrating, humbling. Lasted a very little time. *Far*
closer than even the best Communions. Yet the troubling
part is, I remain hateful; only with vivid efforts can I control
impatience; even today, after this, found people irritating and
failed to be genial and responsive. This would be the greatest
argument against genuineness; but on the other hand, it's nothing
I do—a pure grace—perhaps just because *I* do need it so.

MARCH 18, 1923

Today my God and Joy I felt and knew Thee, Eternal,
Unchanging, transfusing all things, and most wholly and
perfectly given to us in Christ—our in-dwelling with Him a
Total Surrender to Thee—Thyself in all, the one medium of
our union—at Communion to find and love Thee in each
soul to which Thou hast given Thyself.

To know and find Thee, actually and substantially, in all
nations and races and persons—*this* nourishes love and solves

the intercession problem. "Not grace alone, nor us alone, but Thy Grace in us." To *use* and cultivate it. I think the parable of the talents meant this. How far beyond anything one conceived the mysteries seem to stretch now.

The more vivid the vision of Christ grows and the more insistent the demand for dedication, the more one can escape by this path from the maze of self-occupation. He draws, and we run after.

RETREAT: MAY 4–8, 1923

4*th*. I've begun this retreat without much fervor—only just escaping another of those paralyzing fits of doubt. No clear sense of God's Presence—very tired—lately many obscurities and a sort of deadness. I feel less keen all round—not so ardently loving to the poor—sometimes quite an effort to be interested in them. But determined to slog on. Have got to start definitely learning God is in darkness for me as well as light. I've *nothing* at the present moment that the most ordinary small-beer piety couldn't contrive.

Prayer: The Good Shepherd leaning over to save the sheep, clings with *one* hand to the Rock, rescues with the other. So must we. Perhaps the secret of intercession is just this outstretching to others *while* we adhere to God?

Put my whole profession out of sight while here. This is my moment of Communion with God. I think He requires of me a willing entrance into the night of sense, detachment from consolations. Horribly difficult: still, my will is absolutely fixed.

Short general examination. Rows of sins, faults, and tendencies under Pride, Envy, and Anger—don't *see* any yet under Lust, Gluttony, Sloth—probably because I'm not yet *nearly* particular enough.

May 6th, Sunday

The pain of obscurity went last night at Compline. Afterwards I went alone on to the roof, in great peace and acceptance though without vivid awareness—just thinking Christ too prayed like that: high up alone, out of doors at night—one comes closest . . . to His ideal prayer. Gave a sense of complete smallness and peaceful resignation: deep quiet and a kind of return to joy. Made my Communion in great peace and surrender to Christ—without strain—with great sense of the completeness of God's coming down and into things to us—all the Baron means by this came quite gently into me as a solid truth—and after all *nothing* asked from me, but love and a complete sense of my own lowliness. The subtle realism of all the simplest things—if only one could make people see that. Feel more and more the best penitence for me is the general abjection and dependence on Christ, not niggling about special faults, but constant acknowledgement of falling short in love.

May 7th, Monday

The silence ended this morning. Thou hast shown thyself to me, O Christ, coming to me in the humblest duties. Thou hast shown me Thy hidden life—Nazareth and what this shall mean to me. This is the clear path and right sphere of mortification for *me*. I shall reduce even such apparent work for Thee as conflicts with this, and try to fit myself for my service of humble acts of kindness and love. This I have accepted and Thou hast shone on that acceptance. I *know* it is right. Thy subtle and mysterious presence is in this, and if I reject this, all my work for Thee will be wrong. Keep this resolution firm in me. This path, if I can keep on it, is full of Thy light: it means love, repentance, satisfaction, self-denial, faith—all graces in which I conspicuously fail. I promise not to be deflected by people telling me I have a "message," etc. I have nothing at all of value save what Thou dost directly give, and now Thou doest give this priceless opportunity of real self-immolation. Since I saw it, I am utterly and completely quiet and happy so I know if I can do it, it is right.

P.M. I see clearly it's *total*, unconditional self-annihilation which is asked of me and I know I shall never do it—never, in this life.

It all goes back to the day I heard the Voice; all the holy, deepened intimacy of this retreat is a following-out of that really.

May 8th, Tuesday. My last day.

Fruits of this Retreat. An enriched consciousness of Our Lord. A little increase of light about intercession; greater sense of interpenetration with other souls. Renewal of joy, fervor, fixity of intention: fresh nerve for difficult or dreary bits. Clear sense of mortifications already here waiting for me, and resolution not to shirk them and hunt about for others. Have been distinctly shown my immediate duty—more home, kindness, love, and service, whatever sacrifice of work or personal preferences involved. The whole outlook, in the moments of best vision, becomes wider, deeper, more painful, more entrancing. Keep me, O Christ, thus centered on Thee.

1923

Evelyn's relationship with her spiritual director, Baron von Hügel, is discussed in the introduction. The letter she wrote him in the summer of 1923 is a lucid self-evaluation of her personal spiritual life.

From a letter to Baron von Hugel, June, 1923
More steady on my knees though not yet very steady on my feet. Not so rushing up and down between blankness and vehement consolations. Still much oscillation, but a kind of steady line persists instead of zigzags.

I have been trying all the time to shift the focus from feeling to will, but have not yet fully done it, and shall not feel safe till I have. The Christocentric side has become so much deeper and stronger—it nearly predominates. I never dreamed it was like this. It is just beginning to dawn on me what the Sacramental life really does involve: but it is only in flashes of miraculous penetration I can realize this. On the whole, in spite of blanks, times of wretched incapacity, and worse (see below) I have never known such deep and real happiness, such a sense of at last having got my real permanent life, and being able to love without stint, where I am meant to love. It is as if one were suddenly liberated and able to expand all round. Such joy that it sometimes almost hurts. All this, humanly speaking, I owe entirely to you. Gratitude is a poor dry word for what I feel about it. I can't say anything.

The moral struggle is incessant, but there is a queer joy in it. I don't think I need bother you much about that. Small renunciations are easier, but real ones still mean a fight. Nervous tension or exhaustion means a renewed attack of all my old temptations at full strength, and I feel invaded by hard, exasperated, critical, hostile, gloomy, and unloving inclinations.

Of course my will does not consent to these horrors: I do struggle with them: all the same they creep into my mind, and stick for days, another proof at bottom I am un-Christian still (for surely mere nervous tension should not mean these odious feelings?). And that lovely gentle suppleness and radiance I see in all my real Christian friends, and long for, I can't get. I don't think I have ever seen the deepest roots in myself of pride and self-love.

Many religious practices I still can't do, e.g. self-examination. I did make myself do a long written one at my retreat, which perhaps I ought to send you. It looked horrid— but somehow I can't feel much interest in it, or that these curry combings matter much. So much more worth while and far more humbling, just to keep on trying to look at Christ. I know instantly by that when I do anything odious. Even before Holy Communion I don't do much else but, as it were, let that love flow over and obliterate everything. There is so little difference between one's best and worst.

Probably I ought to tell you this. Last October, one day when I was praying, quite suddenly a Voice seemed to speak to me—with tremendous staccato sharpness and clearness. It only said one short thing, first in Latin and then in English! Please don't think I am going in for psychic automatisms or horrors of that sort. It has never happened again, and I don't want it to. Of course I know all about the psychological aspect and am not *hallucinated*. All the same, I simply cannot believe that there was not something deeper, more real, not me at all, behind. The effect was terrific. Sort of nailed me to the floor for half an hour, which went as a flash. I felt definitely called out and settled, once for all—that any falling back or leaving off, after that, will be an unpardonable treason. That sense has persisted—it marked a sort of turning point and the end of all the remorse and worry, and banging about. I feel now if all consolations went it ought not to matter very much, though as a matter of fact derelictions are more painful and trying than they used to be, but have their purifying side. I feel a total, unconditioned dedication is what is asked and it is so difficult. I shall never do it—one fails at every corner.

There have been other things since from time to time, but quite formless, and unspeakably sacred, penetrating, intimate, abasing. Now and then new lights, too, sort of intellectual intuitions, and quite clear of "sensible devotion"; but they are so quick and vast one can only retain about half. I would like to get away from the more vividly emotional feelings: I don't altogether trust them—but how can one help feeling pretty intensely. One has only one soul and body to do one's feelings with after all.

Prayer, at good times though still mixed, is more passive: a sort of inarticulate communion, or aspirations, often merely one word, over and over. Sometimes I wonder whether this is not too much taking the line of least resistance; but it is so wonderful, sweeps one along into a kind of warm inhabited darkness and blind joy—one lives in Eternity in that—can't keep at this pitch long, twenty minutes or so.

I do try to say a few psalms each day and do Intercessions, but one forgets everything then. Of course it's not always like this, often all distraction and difficulty.

As to Intercession, if I ask myself whether I would face complete Spiritual deprivation for the good of another: e.g. to effect a conversion, I can't do that yet. So I have not got real Christian love: and the question is, can one intercede genuinely for anyone, unless ready to pay, if necessary, this price.

Special points (a) A terrible, overwhelming suspicion that after all, my whole "invisible experience" may be only subjective. There are times (of course when one has got it) when it seems incredible that these things could happen to me, considering what I have been. All the books say in unmortified beginners they are very suspicious, so what is one to think?

And further, there is the obvious fact that consolation and deprivation are somehow closely connected with the ups and downs of one's nervous and even bodily life. There is no real test: I may have deceived myself right through, and always studying these things, self-suggestion would be horribly easy. These doubts are absolute torture after what has happened. They paralyze one's life at the roots, once they lodge in the mind. I do not want to shirk *any* pain, but this does not seem a purifying kind. I have read over and over all you say in the Mystical Element—one must have suffering and in a way I wish for it, but I don't get any certitude for myself. The one hopeful side is, what happens, though recognizable, does not really match the books; it does not seem my own, yet *infinitely* transcending anything I could ever have imagined for myself—and grows in depth, mystery, and sweetness.

You said the first time of all, it was all right, I need have no doubts. You know me better now—if you could and would say you still feel absolutely sure, I think I could accept that once for all, and turn my back on all these horrors whenever they come. So far I have struggled through all right, generally by deliberate forced prayer—but this only shelves the problem, does not solve it—and it makes one feel horribly unsafe. The return to peace and certitude is wonderful; but how am I to know for certain this is not just some psychic mechanism? There are times when I wish I had never heard of psychology.

(b) Sometimes an even more terrifying visitation, when not *only* my own inner experience, but the whole spiritual scheme seems in question. The universe seems cast iron and the deterministic view the obvious one. All the old difficulties come back, and especially that chasm between the universal and the historic experience of Christ. I see clearly that for me religious realism is the only thing that is any use. Generally I seem to have it with an increasingly vivid sense of real approach to, or communion with God and Christ as objective facts, completely other than myself. I can't love on any other basis than this: even human love can't be spun from one's dreams and this is far, far beyond that. But in these black times of doubt, it seems possible that one's hours of prayer and adoration simply react on oneself and produce the accompanying experiences. I have no guarantee of genuineness. It is not the awful moral struggle I knew I should have once I gave in; that has a sort of joy in it, those mental conflicts are just pure horror. . . .

Psycho-physical tangles. The parallels between nervous states and spiritual sensitiveness worry me: nerves and soul seem hopelessly mixed up; one thinks one is out of grace and finds it was only mental fatigue and impotence. Don't know how best to run my devotional life in nervous exhaustion. Often too stupefied to think, will, or love at all. I do keep my whole rule somehow—merely kneeling on a hard floor the proper time seems better than nothing—but the struggle to pray is fruitless then. This rule keeping tends to a sort of rigidity. I am restless and starved when my particular routine is upset. And during holidays, or when traveling, lecturing, etc., approximately a quarter of the year—I can't rely on keeping it. Often no privacy, no certain free time safe from interruption: and the desperate struggle to get it at all costs induces a strain which is hostile to prayer. Lately, in fact, "holidays" have been periods of misery on this account. Of course, I never sacrifice Communions unless they are quite impossible—even these I cannot be sure of when we are yachting. What I want here is permission to be more flexible about the external rule and make up by taking every opportunity of quietude or of short aspirations, for any irregularity in long recollections. I believe I should do better like this, and am sure it would not mean slackness. And there must be some way of supernaturalizing one's active life when one can't have one's usual solitude and fixed adoration. After all it's not my choice that I have to be at other people's disposal the whole time. Could not one turn these conditions into something worth offering?

Retreat. May I go to two three-day retreats in the year instead of the one whole-week retreat which you allowed but which is so difficult to manage? *Please* say yes to this! It is such a help and refreshment in one's driving, incessantly active life! I come back completely renovated. But a year between is a long time to wait.

Vocation. I feel great uncertainty as to what God chiefly wants of me. Selection has become inevitable. I can't meet more than half the demands made. I asked for more opportunity of personal service and have thoroughly been taken at my word!

But there is almost no time or strength left now for study for its own sake; I am always giving or preparing addresses, advice, writing articles, trying to keep pace with work, going on committees and conferences—and with so little mental food I risk turning into a sort of fluid clergyman! More serious, the conflict between family claims and duties and work is getting acute. My parents are getting old: they don't understand, and are a bit jealous of the claims on my life (especially as it's all unpaid work). I feel perhaps I ought to have more leisure for them, though I do see them nearly every day. But this could only be done by reducing what seems like direct work for God, or my poor people or something. I confess the work and the poor people are congenial: and idling about chatting and being amiable, when there is so much to be done, is a most difficult discipline—so I can't judge the situation fairly. It is not a case of being needed in any practical sense: just of one's presence being liked, and one's duties slightly resented!

Disobedience. When I have been alone and have had the opportunity, I have sometimes gone to Holy Communion oftener than you said. Otherwise I believe I have kept on my collar and chain.

Guilds of Prayer. Constantly being urged to join Guilds of Prayer, Intercession, etc., and reproached for refusal. Ought I to? I do so want to keep free and hidden in prayer: feel very reluctant to take on these extra rules—but don't wish to be unsocial.

More Journaling from the "Green Notebook"

June 2, 1923

If I ask myself whether I am ready to face complete spiritual deprivation for the good of another—to lose all contact with

Christ, all joy of prayer—give up my deepest life, e.g., that Hilda might find Thee—I can't do that yet. So I have not yet got *really* Christian love. And the question is, can one successfully intercede for the conversion of another, unless one is ready to pay, if asked, this price?

JUNE 10, 1923

It came over me vividly at Communion today, that the whole of the life of Christ consists and always has in *nothing* at all but giving Himself—to every one who asks—pleasant or not—dingy beasts like me—*any*one—making no demands back, cultivating no heavenly joy for Himself—an eternal Risen Life of self-outpouring. It may sound obvious but when you see it, it's pretty overwhelming.

JUNE 20, 1923

Begin to realize now what the sacramental life is, and implies—that it just is, as St. Paul felt, "Christ in you"—His Spirit actually poured into one's soul, being in it, activating it, backing it up—always *there* to be appealed to. So, the strange intimate sense of union which comes now and again involves, really, a sinking down into one's own depths where He is. In loving Him, it *is* God one loves—more and more deeply I feel this.

Essays

1924

THE ESSENTIALS OF MYSTICISM
AND OTHER ESSAYS

Ten essays are gathered together in a volume that takes its title from the first in the series, "The Essentials of Mysticism." Two of these refreshing pieces are included in this compilation. The first, "Spiritual Life," is included here. The second, "The House of the Soul" was written five years later and begins on page 156.

From *Spiritual Life*

"Spiritual Life" is a very elastic phrase which can either be made to mean the most hazy religiosity and most objectionable forms of uplift, or be limited to the most exclusive types of contemplation. Yet surely we should not mean by it any of these things, but something which for most of us is much more actual, more concrete—indeed, an essential constituent of all human life worthy of the name. I am not proposing to talk about mystics or anyone who has rare and peculiar religious experience, but simply about ourselves, normal people living the natural social and intellectual life of our time. If we know much about ourselves, I think we must agree that there is something in us which, in spite of all the efforts of a materialistic psychology, is not accounted for either by the requirements of natural life or those of social life, and which cannot altogether be brought within the boundaries of the intellectual and rational life. Though as it develops, the "something" will penetrate and deeply affect all these levels of our existence, we recognize that it is distinct from them. It is an element which is perhaps usually dormant; yet is sometimes able to give us strange joys, and sometimes strange discomforts. It points beyond our visible environment to something else, to a reality which transcends the time-series, and yet to which we, because of the existence of this quality in us, are somehow akin.

By talking of "spirit" or "spiritual life"—terms more allusive than exact—we do not make these facts less mysterious. But we do make it possible to think about them, and consider what they must involve for our view of the nature of reality; what light they cast on the nature of human beings; and finally how this quality which we call "spiritual life" calls us, as spirits, to act. In other words, we are brought up against the three primary data of religion: God, the soul, and the relation between God and the soul. Those three points, I think, cover the main aspects of humanity's life as spirit. They become, as people grow in spiritual awareness and responsiveness, more and more actual to them, and more and more fully incorporated in their experience. And they are all three represented in the life of prayer—which, taken in the widest sense, is the peculiar spiritual activity of human beings.

By prayer, of course, I do not merely mean primitive prayer—the clamor of the childish creature for help, relief, or gifts from beyond—though this survives in us, as all our primitive and instinctive life still survives. I mean the developed prayer of the soul which has taken its Godward life, its link with the Eternal, seriously; has knocked and had a door opened on to a fresh range of experience. Such prayer as that is just as much a human fact as great achievement in music or poetry and must be taken into account in estimating the possibilities of human life.

We begin then with this fact of something in us which points beyond physical life, however complete that physical life may be, and suggests—perhaps in most of us very faintly and occasionally, but in some with a decisive authority—that somehow we are borderland creatures. As human beings, we stand between an order of things which we know very well, to which most of us are more or less adapted and in which we can easily immerse ourselves, and another order, of which we do not know much but which, if we respond to it and develop a certain suppleness in respect of it, can gradually become the most important factor in our lives. We might sum this up by saying that there is in us a fringe-region where human personality ceases to be merely natural and takes up characteristics from another order, yet without losing concrete hold upon what we call natural life. It is in this fringe-region of our being that religion is born. It points to the fact that we need to be met and completed by an order of being, a reality, that lies beyond us. We are in the making; and such significance as we have is the significance of a still unfinished thing.

Of course, in the pitter-patter of temporal existence it is very easy to lose all sense of this otherness and incompleteness of life, this mysterious quality in human nature. Attention, will, and intelligence have all been trained in response to the physical and turn most easily that way. We live too in a time of immense corporate self-consciousness. Modern literature, with its perpetual preoccupation with the details of our emotional and sexual relationships, reflects this. Universals, and our relation to universals, are neglected. Yet without some recognition of our relation to reality, we are only half-human; and if we are alert, we cannot entirely miss all consciousness of the presence and pressure of that reality, that eternal order, however we may represent it to ourselves. The strange little golden intimations of beauty and holiness that flash up through life, however they come, do present a fundamental problem to us. Are these intimations of reality in its most precious aspect, the faint beginnings of an experience, a development of life, towards which we can move? Or are they mere will-o'-the-wisps? Shall we trust them and give them priority, or regard them with the curiosity that borders on contempt?

In other words, is reality spiritual? Is the only concrete reality God, as the mystics have always declared? And is that richly real and living God present to and pressing upon His whole creation, especially His spiritual creation, or is this merely a pious idea? Are humanity's small spiritual experiences testimonies to a vast truth, which in its wholeness lies far beyond us, or not? We have to choose between these alternatives; and the choice will settle the character of our religion and philosophy, and will also color the whole texture of existence, the way we do our daily jobs.

We assume that the first alternative is the true one; that human beings are created spirits still in the making, and can experience a communion with that living God, Spirit of all spirits, who is the Reality of the universe. What we call our religious experiences, are genuine if fragmentary glimpses of this Divine Reality. That belief, of course, lies at the very heart of real Christian theism. In thinking about it, we are not moving off to some peculiar or specialized mystical religion; we are exploring the treasures of our common faith. And the first point that comes out of it for us, I think, is the distinctness and independence of God and of eternal life as realities so wholly other than the natural order and the natural creature that they must be given us from beyond ourselves. A great deal of modern Christianity, especially that type which is anxious to come to terms with theories of emergent evolution and other forms of immanentism, seems to me to be poisoned by a kind of spiritual self-sufficiency which tends to blur this fundamental and humbling distinction between the creature and God, and between the natural and spiritual life.

It perpetually suggests that all we have to do is to grow, develop, unpack our own spiritual suitcases; that nothing need be given us or done to us from beyond.

Were the fullest possible development of their natural resources the real end of human beings, this might be true enough. But all the giants of the spiritual life are penetrated through and through by the conviction that this is not the goal of human existence, that something must be given, or done to them, from the eternal world over-against us, without which humanity can never be complete. They feel, however variously they express it, that for us in our strange borderland situation there must be two orders, two levels of reality, two mingled lives, to both of which we are required to respond—the natural and the spiritual, nature and grace, life towards others and life towards God—and that the life of spirit of which we are capable must come to us before we can go to it. It is surely the true instinct of religion which fills the liturgy with references to something which must be given or poured out on us. "Pour down on us the continual dew of Thy blessing"—"Pour into our hearts such love towards Thee"—"Without Thee we are not able to please Thee." All summed up in the wonderful prayer of St. Augustine: "Give what Thou dost demand; and then, demand what Thou wilt."

So I suppose, from the human point of view, a spiritual life is a life which is controlled by a gradually developing sense of the eternal, of God and His transcendent reality, an increasing capacity for Him, so that our relation to God becomes the chief thing about us, exceeding and also conditioning our relationship with each other. So here the first and second points which we were to consider—what we mean by a spiritual life, and what a spiritual life involves for us—seem to melt into one other. Indeed, it is almost impossible to consider them separately. For what it means for us is surely this: that we are meant, beyond the physical, to contribute to, indeed collaborate in, God's spiritual creation; to be the willing and vigorous tools and channels of His action in time. That is the spiritual life of humanity at its fullest development, the life of all great personalities: saints, artists, explorers, servants of science. It is a life infinite in its variety of expression, but marked by a certain deep, eternal quality, a disinterested zest for perfection, in all its temporal acts.

When we come to make the personal application of these ideas, this view of the relation of our fluid, half-made personalities to God, and ask how, as individuals, we are called to act—and that is the third of the questions with which we started—we see that just in so far as this view of human life is realistic, it lays on each of us a great and a distinct obligation. Though the life of the Spirit comes from God, the ocean of our being, we have to do something about it. Utter dependence on God must be balanced by courageous initiative. Each of us has a double relationship and is required to develop a double correspondence: first with the Divine Creative Spirit who penetrates and supports our spirits; and secondly with the universe of souls, which is enlaced with us in one vast web of being—whether our immediate neighbors of the Christian family who form with us part of the Mystical Body of Christ, or the more wide-spread corporation of all the children of God, of which this perhaps forms the nucleus.

For those who see life thus, sustained and fed by a present God, and who can say with St. Augustine, "I should not exist were not Thou already with me," the idea of mere self-determination, self-expression as an end in itself, becomes ridiculous. Further than this, the notion of souls, persons, as separate ring-fenced units, is also seen to be impossible. In many ways that are perceptible, and many others so subtle as to be imperceptible, we penetrate and affect one another. The mysterious thing called influence points to our far-reaching power and responsibility and the plastic character of the human self. Because of this plasticity, this interpenetration of spirits, those who have developed their capacity for God, have learnt, as St. John of the Cross says, how to direct their wills vigorously towards Him, can and do become channels along which His life and power can secretly but genuinely transform some bit of life. Devotion by itself has little value, may even by itself be a form of self-indulgence, unless it issues in some costly and self-giving action of this kind.

The spiritual life of any individual, therefore, has to be extended both vertically to God and horizontally to other souls; and the more it grows in both directions, the less merely individual and therefore the more truly personal it will be. It is, in the truest sense, in humanity that we grow by this incorporation of the spiritual and temporal, the deeps and the surface of life, getting more not less rich, various and supple in our living out of existence. Seen from the spiritual angle, Christian selves are simply parts of that vast organism, the Church Invisible, which is called upon to incarnate the divine life in history, and bring eternity into time. Each one of us has his or her own place in this scheme, and each is required to fulfill a particular bit of that plan by which the human world is being slowly lifted Godward, and the Kingdom of God is brought in. This double action—interior and ever-deepening communion with God and, because of it, ever-widening outgoing towards the world as tools and channels of God, the balanced life of faith and works, surrender and activity—must always involve a certain tension between the two movements. Nor, as St. Paul saw, should we expect the double movement to be produced quite perfectly in any one individual, not even in the saints. The body has many members, some of them a very funny shape but each with their own job. The person of prayer and the person of action balance and complete one another. Every genuine vocation must play its part in this transformation in God of the whole complex life of humanity.

Humans are the only created beings of which we have knowledge, who are aware of this call, this need of putting themselves in one way or another at the disposal of Creative Spirit; and this characteristic, even though it is only occasionally developed to the full in human nature, assures us that there is in that nature a certain kinship with God. So every human soul without exception, because of its mysterious affinity with God, and yet its imperfect status, its unlikeness from God, is called to undertake a growth and a transformation that will make of it a channel of the divine energy and will. Such a statement as this, of course, is not to be narrowed down and limited to that which we call the "religious" life. On the contrary it affirms the religious character of all full life. For it means a kind of self-oblivious faithfulness in response to all the various demands of circumstance, the carrying through of everything to which one sets one's hand, which is rooted in a deep—though not necessarily emotional—loyalty to the interests of God. That conception expands our idea of the religious life far beyond the devotional life, till there is room in it for all the multiple activities of human beings in so far as they are prosecuted in, for, and with the Fact of all facts, God-Reality.

I need not point out that for Christians the incarnation— the entrance of God into history—and its extension in the Church bring together these two movements in the soul and in the human complex and start a vast process, to which every awakened soul which rises above self-interest has some contribution to make. As we become spiritually sensitive, and more alert in our response to experience, I think we sometimes get a glimpse of that deep creative action by which we are being brought into this new order of being, more and more transformed into the agents of spirit and able to play our part in the great human undertaking of bringing the whole world nearer to the intention of God. We then perceive the friction of circumstance, the hard and soft of life, personal contacts and opportunities, love and pain and dreariness, to be penetrated and used by a Living Influence, which is making by this means both changes and positive additions to our human nature—softening, deepening, enriching, and molding the raw material of temperament into something nearer the Artist's design.

Next, let us look for a moment at prayer as the special reflection and expression of this relation of God and soul of which we have been thinking. Prayer is, if not the guarantee, at least a mighty witness to the reality of the spiritual life. If we were merely clever animals, had no kinship with God, we could not pray: no communion between Him and us would be possible. Prayer, in its three great forms of worship, communion, and intercession, is after all a purely spiritual activity, an acknowledgement of the supreme reality and power of the spiritual life in human beings. As St. Thomas says, it is a "marvelous intercourse between Infinite and finite, God and the soul!"

If the first aim of the spiritual life is recognition in some way or other of the splendor and reality of God, the first mood of prayer—the ground from which all the rest must grow—is certainly worship, awe, adoration, delight in that holy reality for its own sake. This truth has lately returned to the foreground of religious thought; and there is little need to insist on it afresh. Religion, as von Hügel loved to say, *is* adoration: humanity's humble acknowledgement of the transcendent, the fact of God—the awestruck realism of the seraphs in Isaiah's vision—the meek and loving sense of mystery which enlarges the soul's horizon and puts us in our own place. Prayer, which is so much more a state and condition of soul than a distinct act, begins there, in the lifting of the eyes of the little creature to the living God, or perhaps to the symbol through which the living God reveals Himself to the soul.

It is mainly because we are unaccustomed to a spiritual outlook which is centered on the infinite mystery of God and not merely on ourselves and our own needs and desires, that we so easily become confused by the changes and chances of experience. And for modern people, confronted as we all are by a swiftly changing physical and mental universe sweeping away as it must many old symbolic constructions but giving in their place a fresh and humbling sense of the height and depth and breadth of creation and our own small place in it, it is surely imperative to establish and feed this adoring sense of the unchanging reality of God. It is easy, so long as the emphasis lies on us and our immediate interests, to be baffled and depressed by a sense of our own futility. Our whole life may seem to be penned down to attending to the horrid little tea-shop in the valley, yet this and every other vocation is ennobled if we find time each day to lift our eyes to the everlasting snows. I think we might make far greater efforts than we do to get this adoring remembrance of the reality of God, who alone gives our work significance, woven into our everyday lives. There is no more certain method of evicting pettiness, self-occupation, and unrest, those deadly enemies of the spiritual self.

It is within this penetrating sense of God present yet transcendent, which at once both braces and humbles us, that the second stage of prayer—a personal self-giving that culminates in a personal communion—emerges and grows. Here we have the personal response and relationship of the self to that God who has evoked our worship. Adoration, as it more deeply possesses us, inevitably leads on to self-offering, for every advance in prayer is really an advance in love. "I ask not for thy gifts but for thyself," says the divine voice to Thomas à Kempis. There is something in all of us which knows that to be true. True, because of the fact of human freedom: because human beings have the awful power of saying Yes or No to God and His purposes, linking up our separate actions with the great divine action or pursuing a self-centered or earth-centered course. This is the heart of practical religion, and can be tested on the common stuff of our daily lives. It is this fact of freedom which makes sacrifice, with its elements of personal cost and confident approach and its completion in communion, the most perfect symbol of the soul's intimate and personal approach to God. If worship is the lifting up towards the Infinite the eyes of faith, self-offering is the prayer of hope: the small and fugitive creature giving itself, its thoughts, deeds, desires in entire confidence to the mysterious purposes of eternal life. It is summed up in the great prayer of St. Ignatius, "Take, Lord, and receive!"

But as the realistic sense of God in Himself which is the basis of adoration leads on to a realistic personal relationship with Him in self-offering and communion, so from this self-offering and communion there develops that full and massive type of prayer in which spiritual power is developed and human creatures become fellow workers with the Spirit, tools and channels through which God's creative work is done. That is the life of charity, the life of friendship with God for which we were made. Growth in spiritual personality means growth in charity. And charity—energetic love of God, and of all people in God—operating in the world of prayer, is the live wire along which the power of God, indwelling our finite spirits, can and does act on other souls and other things, rescuing, healing, giving support and light. That, of course, is real intercession, which is gravely misunderstood by us if we think of it mainly in terms of asking God to grant particular needs and desires. Such secret intercessory prayer ought to penetrate and accompany all our active work if it is really to be turned to the purposes of God. It is the supreme expression of the spiritual life on earth: moving from God to human beings, through us, because we have ceased to be self-centered units but are woven into the great fabric of praying souls, the "mystical body" through which the work of Christ on earth goes on being done.

We talk about prayer thus by means of symbols; but as a matter of fact we cannot really rationalize it without impoverishing it. It leads us into the world of mystery where the Creative Spirit operates, in ways beyond and above all we can conceive, yet along paths which touch and can transform at every point our humble daily lives and activities. Thus prayer, as the heart of our spiritual life—our Godward response and striving—is seen to be something which far exceeds devotional exercises and is and must be present in all disinterested striving for perfection, for goodness, for truth and beauty, or for the betterment of the children of God. For it means the increasing dedication and possession of all our faculties by Him, the whole drive of our active will subdued to His design, penetrated by His life, and used for His ends.

And last, coming down to ourselves, how does all this work out in the ordinary Christian life? It works out, I think, as a gradual growth in the soul's adherence to God and co-operation with God, achieved by three chief means: 1. Discipline, menial, moral, and devotional. 2. Symbolic and sacramental acts. 3. Ever-renewed and ever more perfect dedication of the will, death to self. This point, of course, is incomparably the most important. The others have their chief meaning in the fact that they contribute to and support it.

Discipline. This includes the gradual training of our faculties to attend to God, by the regular practice of meditation and recollected vocal prayer. Also such moral drill as shall conduce to the conquest of the instinctive nature, the triumph of what traditional asceticism calls the "superior faculties of the soul" or, in plain English, getting ourselves thoroughly in hand. At least, in the experience of most souls, this will involve a certain moderate amount of real asceticism, a painful effort to mortify faults of character, especially those which are ramifications of self-love, and a humble submission to some elementary education in devotional routine. Under this heading we get an ordered rule of life, voluntary self-denials, and a careful detachment of the emotions from all overwhelming attractions which compete with God. Acceptance of the general methods and regulations of the Church also comes in here, as the first stage in that very essential process, the socializing and incorporation of the individual life of prayer so that it may find its place, and make its contribution to the total life of the Mystical Body of Christ. None of this is actual prayer, but all of it, in various degrees, must enter into the preparation of the self for prayer.

Next, *symbolic acts.* Even if we can dare to say that there is such a thing as an absolute and purely spiritual communication of God with the soul (and such a mystically inclined theologian as von Hügel thought that we could not say this), such absolute communications are at best rare and unpredictable flashes and, even where they seem to us to happen, are confined to the highest ranges of spiritual experience. They could never form its substance; and it would be an intolerable arrogance on our part—a departure from creatureliness bringing its own punishment with it—if we planned our inner life on such lines. We are sense-conditioned, and must use the senses in our approach to God, accepting the humbling truth that His absolute being is unknowable and can only be apprehended by us under symbols and incarnational veils. This of course is both Christianity and common sense.

But as well as this, we have to acknowledge that the real nature of His work within the soul is also unknowable by us. When we enter the phase of suffering, this truth becomes specially clear. Only by its transforming action within the mental or volitional life, purifying, illuminating, stirring to fervor or compelling to sacrifice, can we recognize the creative working of God. And even these inward experiences and acts, vital as they are for us, are still only symbolic in their conveyance of God. Récéjac's celebrated definition of mysticism as "the tendency to approach the Absolute morally and by means of symbols" covers, when we properly understand it, the whole spiritual life of human beings, for the ground of the soul where His Spirit and our freedom meet is beyond the reach of our direct perceptions. There is therefore no realistic religion for the human creature which is not expressed in symbolic acts. We cannot cut our world into two mutually exclusive parts and try to achieve the Infinite by a rejection of the finite. And when and if those more profound and really mystical depths of prayer are reached where we seem indeed to be subdued to a presence and action which has no image, and of which we can say nothing at all—when the eternal background has become the eternal environment and we are sunk in God—then that very sense of an entire passivity which accompanies the soul's deepest action, of being, as Jacopone says, "drowned in the Divine Sea," is surely one more tribute to the part played by symbolism in the normal process of the spiritual life.

And last, the essence of that life, *dedication of the will.* This of course is the ever-deepening temper of all personal religion worthy of the name. In its first movement it constitutes conversion; in its achieved perfection it is the very substance of the unitive life of the saint. But between those two points there is much work to be done and much suffering to be borne by those in whom this self-transcendence, this supernatural growth, is taking place. Because of the primary importance of God's overruling action, and yet also the great importance of the self's free and willing activity, there must be within any full spiritual life, at least until its final stages, a constant tension between effort and abandonment, loving communion and ethical struggle, illumination and purification, renunciation of the will and deliberate use of the will, as the natural and supernatural aspects of personality, both invaded and subdued to the divine purpose, come into play and the will of God for that soul is expressed in calls to concrete activity or to inward abandonment. So too in the actual life of prayer we ought to expect, and practice in some degree, both the deliberate effort of intercession and the abandoned quiet of contemplation. And as the soul grows in suppleness under these alternating stimulations—these "stirrings and touches of God," as the mystics so realistically call them—so its sense of the divine action, which is always there but not always recognized, becomes more distinct and individuated until at last, in the full theopathetic life of the mystical saint, it becomes a perfectly responsive tool of the creative will. "I live yet not I." That of course is a real statement of experience, not a piece of piety; an experience which is reflected in the abnormal creative activities and spiritual power of the saints, from Paul of Tarsus to the *Curé d'Ars*.

And with this, I think, we reach the answer to the question with which we began: What exactly is the spiritual life? It is the life in which God and His eternal order have, more and more, their undivided sway; which is wholly turned to Him, devoted to Him, dependent on Him, and which at its term and commonly at the price of a long and costly struggle, makes the human creature a pure capacity for God. And as regards the actual prayer, the secret correspondence which accompanies this growth, this will tend mainly to fulfill itself along two paths: upwards to God in pure adoration—

outward to the world in intercession. The interweaving of these two movements in the special way and degree in which they are developed by each soul, is the foundation of the spiritual life of humanity.

CONSCIOUSNESS OF GOD: FROM "THE GREEN NOTEBOOK"

OCTOBER 31, 1923

I begin to think that the most profound effects of the Peace of God are manifested in the subconscious—it's the quieting of this that delivers one from anxiety and unrest. This accounts for the fact that though consciousness of God is so often absent, the deep hidden peace never seems really to fail, and wells up gently when the mind is at rest. I wonder whether this, which I have only just discovered by introspection, is what the medievals meant by the "ground of the soul."

ADVENT 1923

This month of illness has been full of a sort of leisured heavenliness—taught me a not intense and vivid, but gentle, constant, and peaceful dwelling in the Presence of God. Quite easy to turn to external things without a jolt and then back to Him again. Of course, not contemplation or anything near it, but a very steadying and enlarging sort of thing, and awfully sweet and dear! What a span it is from the pure joy in God's utter transcendence, to the intimacy of the presence of Jesus in the soul—that coming right down to the bottom into the dregs.

More and more I realize what the Baron means by the "Otherness"—in this leisure one *can* get quiet and recollected and make a little progress—my general life's too quick and packed with things—shall never seriously improve in prayer and vision unless I can get stretches of quietude.

DECEMBER 4, 1923

Today, abruptly, in five minutes of prayer I *knew* the Ocean of Love—the "boundless living substance"—through me, and all of us, immersing us, one Love—it's true, "the plural is never found." Incredible joy—one feels in such a moment, one could never allow oneself an act or feeling below this—that anything but love is impossible—because it's *all* and all GOD—but I *shall* incessantly fall into separateness again. How wonderful that weak and rotten little creatures like me can see this even though one can't "sustain one's gaze."

DECEMBER 26, 1923

Looking back on this autumn I feel I have chiefly learnt two things:

1. A deep and clear sense of the all-penetrating Presence of God and of Love as His deepest nature—or at least the nearest *we* can come to it: and so, of any decent thing we do as *not* ours, but a direct activity of the one Love, passing right through and vivifying one, like the sea waters supporting and passing right through a shell fish. Yet, all the time, one remains one's own beastly self! Great deepening and enrichment of one's sense of God at times—but it slips away; I can't hold it.

2. More and more I realize, the union with Christ one craves for can and must be only through union with His redemptive work, always going on in the world. If I ever hesitate before this, the pain and stress it must mean for us wretched little creatures used as His instruments—then I draw back from Him and break the link. So the "life of

supremely happy men" is *not* "alone with the alone"—it's the redeeming life, now and in Eternity, too, in ever greater and more entrancing union with the Spirit of Jesus ceaselessly at work in the world. Only one must have the quiet times, too, to consolidate that union and stretch-out the house of one's soul, and feed on Him.

1923

"OUR TWOFOLD RELATION TO REALITY"

From Hibbert Journal, January, 1925

The devotee and the practical man alike represent subtractions from the richness of human life. For the devotee, if he turns away from the visible and contingent, is failing to accept those humbling lessons and homely opportunities, those strains and tests in which it abounds: whilst the practical man is still more hopelessly divorced from full experience, for he fails to look beyond the contingent to that assigned end which alone gives it meaning and puts us in a position to deal with it properly. He flagrantly disobeys the first and great commandment of the Gospel—the Charter of spiritual life. Thou shalt love the Lord thy God with all thy Heart and with all thy Soul and with all thy Mind and with all thy Strength. . . . For the individual, this means making a place in our flowing life for a deliberate self-orientation to the Eternal Order. For the community it means providing an environment in which these interests can be cherished and taught. Religion in its special language calls these two essentials of full life Prayer and Church. But the values and needs which they represent are deeply rooted in the facts of human nature, and stretch far beyond the narrow meaning commonly attached to them, and the crystallized form they have been allowed to assume.

SELF EVALUATION
FROM: "THE GREEN NOTEBOOK"

JANUARY 15, 1924

I don't think God will ever make me good: what He wants is
to use me as a tool, to reach others and do His work in them.
But in the end probably my sort is for the dust heap. If His
purposes are advanced and one does what He calls for, one
ought not really to mind this. I doubt whether intellectual
keenness and speculation are ever fully compatible with
sanctity. Meanwhile he is my joy, and Eternal Life is a present
fact and the sense of His immense reality and penetrative
presence keeps on deepening; folds me up in prayer in a
wonderful silvery light and quietness and seems quite to
extinguish the desire and need for vivid consolations.

JANUARY 25, 1924

I don't improve *one bit* in charity. Today for a bit, suddenly and
as it were forcing one into prayer, not a silvery light but a
wonderful golden glow—and within this glow of God one
sees Jesus. A sort of musical sense of adoration fills one
then—nothing else at all but worship and delight. Had been
to Communion feeling very dead and undevout two hours
previously.

FEBRUARY 8, 1924

Do feel lately a bit more as if I had got my feet on the
ground. Recently that deeply quiet prayer, as if one just
keeps still and the presence of God wraps one right up in a
sort of velvety rest, comes of itself when one begins: though
not of course always. When it does, there's no effort of over
aim—it's all just as St. Teresa says, complete, simple, and

naturally supernatural. I feel less and less distinction between times of prayer and times of activity within and for God: and this, though I remain very bad at aspirations, horribly blown about by temptations to exasperation, hardness, and lack of charity, and generally not one bit better. But direction work is done now by something not me, which tells me exactly what to say.

In the middle of last night, when I was broad awake, something wonderful happened—a real disclosure—convincing, complete. It's all completely gone but what St. Augustine called "the fragrance"—but it showed in the loveliest way the real relation between all our symbols and images and the Reality, and that the symbols and images *were* perfectly all right and truly in it. A sort of infinite loveliness and color and quiet joy. One is *so* tiny and *so* much nothing—that the question of one's own awful imperfectness doesn't come in. There it is, in a sort of eternal ruling beneficence, and now and then one gets a glimpse.

A consummate leader of spiritual retreats, Evelyn Underhill was offered more opportunities to lead retreats than she could accept. A number of her retreats are now published, demonstrating how one growing soul relates with others to their mutual benefit.

1924

SANCTITY: THE PERFECTION OF LOVE

RETREAT TEXT, MARCH 15, 1924

Too many people come to a retreat possessed of the idea that most of the time is to be spent exploring, examining themselves. Very often, going in with this idea, they come out in the exhausted state of women who have been to a remnant sale. They are weary and distracted with overhauling rubbish and things that don't matter: considering a particular fault and whether it's been substantially reduced, wondering whether a certain achievement is quite worth the price put on it. What does all this matter?

Remember what our Lord said to Julian of Norwich when she was inclined to be fussy: "Take it generally!" That's the voice of wisdom—quietly ignoring the importance we attach to our little selves. Once for all, tonight, let us turn our backs on our niggling self-scrutiny. Let us look at God, at Christ. That will bring us to a state of mind more humbling, more really contrite than any penitence based only on introspection. It will condemn every failure in love. "My soul *opened*" said Lucie-Christine, not "my soul turned *inwards* and began to look at itself through a microscope"!

Now I don't mean to discredit all self-examination. It must have a place in the soul's life. But do take it generally, in a broad spirit. Let it be examination of motive rather than of act. Let it be swift, all 'round stock taking: review of needs, weaknesses, habits, and difficulties here in the quiet before God. And do it with gratitude to Him, not with horror. Remember, our difficulties of character, our unspiritual instincts, are material given us for sanctification.

Be patient. It is wrong to speak of "our dreadful nature." It is the nature that Christ took. The sight of faults and deficiencies are a grace; they are shown us by God. We can't find them alone. . . .

PEACE

Peace is, above all things, a state of the will. It is a calm, willed acceptance of all the conditions which God imposes upon us and which deepens with our deepening realization of Him. The things which work against it are four forms of wanting our own way, four kinds of disharmony between our will and the will of God. And that which conquers these four kinds of self-will for us is the fourth suggestion made by à Kempis: that we "desire ever and pray that the will of God be all and wholly done." When we thus completely transfer the center of interest from our ideas to His ideas, then we indeed enter the coasts of peace and quiet.

This peace, which St. Paul says must crown our love and our joy if they are genuine, is not merely a nice religious feeling that comes to us in times of prayer. It does not mean basking in the divine sunshine like comfortable pussycats. It is a peace that needs and indeed produces a courageous and yet humble kind of love. It means such a profound giving of ourselves to God, such an utter neglect of our own opinions, preferences, and rights, as keeps the deeps of our souls within His atmosphere in all the surface rush, the ups and downs, demands and disappointments, joy and suffering of daily life. We cease to matter. Only God and His work matters.

He demands an unmeasured love, and His response is an unmeasured peace. "My peace I give unto you." Think what that peace really is!—a peace tested in Gethsemane, in mockery, in insult, misunderstanding, apparent failure, the extremity of pain, yet so radical that it could be given from the Cross to the dying thief. "Not as the world giveth . . ." but as the Crucified giveth, at His own cost, now from beyond the world. If we are really growing towards God, we are growing towards that ideal.

And it is only in such a state of peace as this that our best work can be done. We don't do it in a state of tension and anxiety. We don't hear God's voice then. Worry is one of the most ungodly things in the whole world. We shall do our best work in a deepening spirit of earnestness, responsibility, and a sense of obligation. We shall do our best when we are inspired by that loving longing of the soul to do the last bit we can for God, being wholly swayed by the Spirit that molds and uses us. But we shall not work in agitation or strain. So too with our mental obligations, problems, and difficulties. We are called upon to deal with those problems up to the limit of our understanding, but always in the atmosphere of "the peace that passes understanding."

Again à Kempis says, "Seek ever the lower place." Humbleness, a necessary condition of our love and our joy, is the very substance of our peace. The more our sense of God's infinite reality, His steady mysterious action on life, deepens, the less important we and our little efforts and failures grow, and the greater our peace grows. You see it as the golden thread of humility which links together the three great gifts made to us by the Spirit of God: love, joy, and peace.

If we are not to let our hearts be troubled about our work and its difficulties, even about the sin, failure, and need with which we may be trying to deal, still less are we to let them be troubled about our own souls. Self-occupation of that sort is not so much wrong as idiotic, but it is the kind of idiocy which soon brings decay into the spiritual life. Softening of the soul, which is worse than softening of the brain, sets in. We become religious invalids, always wondering what we can venture to eat, drink, do, or risk—and that sort of personality is miserable stuff to offer God.

Some people are always wondering what is the best thing for their souls, and if you told them that really it did not much matter, they would be shocked. But the best way to manage the soul is much the same as the best way to manage the body. First look at its real needs, real weak points, and real obligations squarely in the face. Prescribe for them if necessary, or get someone else to do it for you. Find out the rule of life that suits you, the work to which you are called, the right way to manage yourself so that you can do this work, and then, having found this out, stick to it.

One of the things which can well be done in retreat is something which everyone who takes spiritual life seriously should do. It is to decide on the balance of prayer, spiritual reading, work, recollection, recreation, and rest which will make us most effective instruments of God's will and help us to live, work, and endure on higher levels. That is the real point, not our particular devotional preferences or daintinesses. That is the road to peace.

Here too an ever deepening and more loving vision of God's greatness and our immaturity will help us to see things in proportion, to realize ourselves, as it were, as seedlings growing in an infinite garden. It will check what St. John of the Cross called "spiritual gluttony." We might call it "spiritual ambition," that fussy envy of people who are doing better than ourselves: all the copycat sort of holiness. If we can see things in proportion, it will make us very willing, even in the things of the Spirit, to have less rather than more, and take the lower place. And we shall grow, expand, and deepen in proportion to the extent to which we achieve this peaceful forgetfulness of ourselves.

Such forgetfulness of self means peace too in the necessary ups and downs of our own spiritual course, accepting here, as elsewhere, that which comes from God. When we can say with no sense of unreality, "If Thou wilt that I be in the light, blessed be Thou. And if Thou wilt that I be in the darkness, blessed be Thou. Light and darkness, life and death, praise ye the Lord," as à Kempis says—if we can really say that, it means that in the deeps of our souls our wills are indeed peacefully united to the holy will and love that guides this little world and gave us the model of the Cross. Merging ourselves in that will, we find our peace.

We think it is rather immature to be upset about the weather, yet very few souls tranquilly pursue the spiritual course without minding the spiritual weather. Here too we must expect fog, cold, persistent cloudiness, gales, and sudden stinging hail, as well as the sun.

We ought not to mind the fact that there are dim, flat, and obscure patches in our religious life. When we come to them, joy may seem to go, but if our love is really a courageous love, peace will remain. Peace can be there even when it seems to us that we are not getting on in the least because we are not seeking our own profit. And we can have peaceful belief in the infinite patience and generosity of God who knows how to wait.

Perfect clearness in religion often really means just shallowness, for, being what we are, we cannot expect to get eternal life into sharp focus. Often indeed God and His peace are more surely present with us in darkness than in light. We ought to be equally ready for both. It is a very poor sort of faith and love that will not face a dark passage until it knows where the switch is.

It is also true that there are moments in the life of communion when the soul doesn't *wish* to see, to fully comprehend. The gift is made so subtly because we can't endure the full daylight glare. It is not in our comprehension, but in God's will, that our peace abides.

Often we hear complete surrender to God spoken of as something that very religious people may possibly attain, but we hardly realize how exceedingly absurd the opposite is. We do not see the hopelessness of setting up our tiny, half-real, half-animal, and altogether infantile wills, swayed by all sorts of silly longings and primitive impulses, against the mighty process of His perfect will. Nor do we recognize the folly of trying to make little whirlpools in the great, steady stream of that creative will and love. How utterly impossible to be happy or harmonized if we do that! His service is perfect freedom, and service means doing things in your master's way and not your own. No service is possible without humility and obedience.

Now you see we have gotten down to the very foundations of love and joy. It is the same law as the law of Paradise which Dante learned and which we have quoted from Augustine: "In His Will is our peace." This is the law which turns the whole world into the Kingdom of Heaven, for peace is a state of the will, and the will, as the old mystics liked to say, is the king of the soul. "Heaven in our souls" then, simply consists in the harmony of our will with God's will. If then, "Heaven is a temper of mind and not a place," heaven is that temper of peaceful surrender which places our wills in perfect harmony with God's.

We have perpetual opportunities, both little and great, of entrance into that heaven. We have chances offered to us of doing hard and boring and self-forgetful things, of accepting the rebuff, the misunderstanding, the sudden disarrangement of plan which comes to us. We have opportunities of going on quietly with our job without recognition, taking all the ruffles of the surface of life just as they come. The result of that is peace, peace even if our outward life does seem a continuous rush, or even a continuous discouragement.

St. Augustine said that we are nothing else but wills: our inner life, that is, is always aiming at something, intending something. Generally it is a self-interested something which attracts and keeps our attention. The result—since God made us for Himself and is the only adequate object of our will—is that we are restless. Different and really incompatible things are pulling at our will and our attention, and the result of this is an interior conflict that saps our strength.

Now it is right and wholesome that we should have varieties of interest, but it must be variety in unity. Yet the unity within which all our differing interests, occupations, and desires are enclosed must be the overruling peace of a will that has been given to God. In the rush of our daily lives, to absent ourselves for a moment, to turn to Him, and to reaffirm that consecration is to recover peace. We all know too well how easily we turn in odd moments to our worries and preoccupations. We should use the same method to pacify, instead of exasperate, our souls.

You remember how the *Pax Romana* embraced and gave security and tranquility to many different nations by freeing them from the burden and exhaustion of war among themselves? They remained different and distinct nations. They kept their own customs, industries, and ideas, but they were harmonized under one steady rule.

So, within the peace of God, we retain our personal and diverse interests and powers, our full variety of life and vocation, but redeemed from conflict. Thus we are able to use the whole of our strength for creation and for service.

It is just as St. Paul, before his conversion, wasted his splendid energy kicking against the pricks. But after his conversion, that stream of power flowed into one channel of creation given to Christ, and he lived in perfect peace one of the hardest lives that a Christian has ever lived. The vision of Christ which he met on the road to Damascus did not reproach Paul with wickedness but with silliness. How hard it is to kick against the goad. What a foolish, wasteful thing to do!

The Spirit of God is always pressing our souls to fulfill His mysterious purpose for each one of us, and our peace consists in obedience to the pressure. Misery and discord come from kicking against it. After his conversion, Paul was always talking about peace, although he seemed to be living a life that most people would consider unpeaceful to the last degree. He begins every letter by wishing his correspondents peace—grace and peace. He wishes them God's presence in their lives, and the tranquility which follows. A sense of power and of quietude comes to us when we read his words. . . .

PRAYER

Prayer is our soul's response to God's immense attraction, and this response begins in the activity of the will. Will and desire are the heart of the mental life turned to God. This is not mere pious reverie. As Saint Teresa says, at the beginning of our prayer life, we have to draw the living water out of the well. It is hard work. We can't leave it to chance. God requires our communion with Him to be an act, an effort, and to cost something. Think of the trouble we give ourselves to get time to be with those whom we love. Is it not ever so much more important to make a way to commune with God?

We are spiritual creatures with the power of communion with God, breathing the air of eternity. We can't keep this power unless we exercise it. Nor can we fully get it unless we train ourselves to it. We must accustom our attention, that wanders over all other interests, to fix itself on Him. Such deliberate attention to God is the beginning of real prayer. Prayer is never to be judged by feeling that goes with it: it is the willed intercourse of our tiny spirits with the Infinite Spirit of Love.

In the life of prayer, our wills and God's grace act together. When we consider what prayer is and what it can become, how *wonderful* that little half-grown creatures like us can have communion with God! We realize that we couldn't do it by our own strength alone. But this doesn't excuse us from using our strength. Teresa got to haul the bucket up. Going limp or having a nice all-overish religious feeling is not prayer; it is not interchange with God. Prayer covers all ways in which our will and love reaches out to one Reality and Love in adoration, longing, penitence, confidence, and joy.

Consider Christ's three *promises* of prayer in Matthew 7:7-8. Note how all of them are attached to something done by us. The question of whether we will commune with God is left to *us*, to the freedom of our wills. God gives out of His treasury what we *really* ask, seek, and long for. His supply is infinite; it is our demands which are shallow, mistrustful, and vague. The saints were so sure about the extent in which human life is a spiritual thing and Spirit-fed that they asked and received *much*.

"Ask," "seek," and "knock": there is something very definite about that. Those words represent three very real stages in the life of prayer corresponding to a steady growth and enrichment of the soul's encounter with God. When we begin real prayer, all of us feel very helpless. We are filled with craving, with longing. We are asking for God. We want assurance, light, spiritual food, strength to carry on and deal with our difficulties and sins. We are met by grief and temptations which we cannot face alone. We begin the terrible struggle up from a mere animal selfish life, and we *must* be helped. We want something to be added to our human nature from the supernatural world if we are to grow up to be children of God. And opening our souls to the spiritual world in prayer, *asking, we do receive*—although perhaps not instantly or sensationally. Perhaps the answer is not exactly what we expect. Still a gift is made, and prayer in the spiritual life becomes possible to us. A response comes from the dim world which surrounds and penetrates us.

The second promise is that if we will seek, we will find. That meditation which is a deep brooding exploration and thinking in God's presence is a way to the real discovery of the spiritual life. Some people are helped by formal meditation. Others can't do it. But there is always some way in which all can seek to know more of God and their own souls. The utmost that we can achieve is only a tiny bit of full reality but more than enough of happiness. Yielding ourselves to God in prayer, gradually discovering bit by bit, often not in big disclosures, is His call to our souls.

We may not be specialists in our vocation to one definite kind of sacrifice or redemptive work in action or in prayer. The Church is not a society of specialists, but of living, loving, ever-growing souls which must stretch up to God in adoration and out to one's companions in active love, doing or not doing ever in accord with God's will and God's voice. One of the great functions of prayer is to train us to this attitude of soul. Seeking His will requires courage, patience, and trust. The deep things of prayer are first given in response to these.

Seeking God in prayer means we have realized that we want Him more than any of His gifts. In seeking in this single-minded way, we discover en route a good deal about ourselves. The woman with the lost piece of silver had to have a complete spring cleaning. She found much dust, but forgot the rubbish and perhaps forgot the treasure too.

That seeking in prayer, like all spiritual processes, must be gentle, not feverish, and unstrained. A method of patience and confidence marks good explorers. In seeking ourselves, there should be no uproar or wild hunting. We need to clean the windows and let in the light. Then like a householder, we find the new and old appropriate to our souls, which help us to slowly deepen and widen our life in Him. Thus acting, at last we *find* ourselves as truly living the life of the Spirit, truly supplied by Love.

We also find our own vocation in this life of prayer. Our vocations vary. Some specialists are appointed for intercession. We develop our power, as the souls of others open, to embrace their lives and needs. Yet not all can do this. Others are drawn to adoration or loving absorption in God. Both types find more and more the homeliness and naturalness of this life with God. Julian said this was the deepest of her discoveries about Him. It was the inward gentleness and humbleness of God's approach to our souls in prayer that St. Teresa referred to as "gentle rain."

For the third promise we are asked to knock. Now comes the time in our prayer when we seem brought up short by a closed door. Generally, we experience the other side of that door, the riches of the house of God. But this is the real life at which all our education in prayer has been gently aiming, life lived in the atmosphere of God beyond entreaty and search. We leave those off when we are at home.

Home—When we realize all that that image implies, don't prayers merely *asking* for help or comfort seem a bit mean and ungenerous? True, they are answered out of the boundless generosity of God, but our aim ought to lie beyond, in a life lived in Him. As we began we sang, "Holy, Holy, Holy!" All that matters is God, not ourselves. This is the attitude to which the life of prayer should bring us. It is St. Paul's attitude of adoration, of delighted surrender.

Knock. Nothing is said about what happens when the door opens. Christ's silence is more eloquent than speech. We needn't suppose that other sorts of prayer are then shut to us. St. John said that the sheep come in and out of the door and find pasture. Adoration brings us to a door, but it is life in the world beyond the door that then overrules all.

Now to some, these thoughts I know will be commonplace. To others, there will be those which are new and strange. We are all in a different class in the school of prayer. It is important not to try to force ourselves to practice one kind of praying when God is teaching us another. Children don't try to do sums in the middle of a music lesson. Nevertheless, it is not uncommon for people whose attraction is to silent communion to struggle to do formal meditation or get through intercession or vocal prayer which they've taken on as a discipline. Do be simple and natural!

To be truly silent before God is one of the loveliest things in the world. It is much like the story to which we referred in our first meeting together, the story of the old man whose prayer was simply looking at God and letting God look at him.

Silence comes of itself. Mechanical silence, the silence for which one struggles, is one of the most sterile of silences. This is why some find corporate silence difficult. They don't know what to do with it. But if each person *attends to God in the way we attend to anyone we deeply love,* instead of attending to the silence or what others are doing—if we just open our souls to God, the result will be all right.

Everyone's contribution is not required to be the same! Get real about it. Live, breathe, open your souls and feed them. Turn to God. You will find Christ offering Himself just in the way *you* can bear it. He will teach you best. And remember Teresa's advice: when you start to pray, get yourself some company as quickly as you can!

Remember also, fixed times of prayer have as their object the building up of a constant state of prayer in which we live and work in God's presence. That alone is a full Christian life. It is hard at first to acquire and keep such a state. Do you recall how Brother Lawrence said that for a long time it brought great difficulty to him? We have to realize that our souls need a long education in prayer. We must expect it and be patient with ourselves.

Much of our prayer is at first a sort of training, and most of us need frequent tuning-up and the help of ideas and phrases that keep us pointed in the right way. If anyone says that this is self-suggestion, I agree. Some of it is. But we ought to suggest to ourselves spiritual ideas. That is a method God has given us. We needn't be afraid of doing what always has been done when we do it under a new name.

Formal prayer makes a direct suggestion to our souls and reminds us of what we always tend to forget. If this were grasped, then the supposed unreality would cease to trouble us. If that proposal is used, it will train us to a sense of God's presence.

Writings on prayer refer to acts and aspirations, little phrases by which, from time to time, we lift up our minds and hearts to God. They are seen as among the most valuable forms of prayer. We should try to accustom ourselves to use them frequently during the day. For example, we can use the Psalms, the Prayer Book, or the *Imitation of Christ*. They are full of aspirations.

These phrases of aspiration and thousands like them slip past us easily. If we stop, dwell, brood, and make food of them, we will find that thus used, they will open to us paths to mental prayer. They bring about levels of devotion wonderful in their claim and demand. They give the mind something to hold onto. They quiet it, but they stir us to feel the love, humility, and adoration which they suggest. In trains and at odd moments, they can lift our hearts to God. Hymns, too, lull distressing thoughts and so gradually educate our thoughts and feeling to run more and more in their channels. Such habits furnish an immediate source of peace and security.

Some individuals have what we would call an aptitude for contemplation. This attitude of mind comes almost naturally. But all of us must feed it and renew it if we wish to keep it fresh and real. We must have the skeleton of a habit. A *rule* of prayer is essential to the life of prayer just as for the sacraments there must be a definite rule of Holy Communion. The rule is not to be forsaken because we feel cold and dead. It is no use to say that our work shall be our prayer. It won't be unless we train our souls and get the color of prayer into it; and this means regular times of total attention to God as well as frequent aspirations.

A Christianity which is only active is not a complete Christianity at all. Christ's times of retirement for communion with his Father prove that. There is a lovely and even homely intimacy of spirit in God, in Christ, which lights up for us not only what we call good works but every sort of creative work. Thus we learn to weave together this world and the Eternal World; and we fill all we do with gentle loveliness which is of God. . . .

PRAYER AND ADORATION

All attempts to narrow prayer down to this or that, to empha-size one aspect against another, to understand its richness and variety are fruitless. I've heard people refer to the "need" for prayer as if there is a sort of electrical current which must be employed to move things, to boil the kettle, to do useful work. This would suggest that the holy energy of God is there to do our jobs instead of us being there to do His. Others say that the loving communion of the Soul with God in prayer is selfish. There are those who contend that to pray for something intimates that we can affect the will of God. Then there are some who are captains of real prayer who get distracted because they find their way of praying not like that of others.

Prayer is our *whole life* of communion with God, whether secret or corporate. If one thinks of it like that, one shall get a richer and deeper view of it. We shan't let ourselves be worried by people with special views about it.

Prayer is the whole life of the Soul. It is the life in which one breathes spiritual air, feeds on spiritual food, learns spiritual things, and does spiritual work. It is not one but *all* these things. It is *life*.

Shall this life be less in contrasting variety, richness, intricate beauty, tension, joy, pain, fellowship, and loneliness than is bodily life on earth? All of these are in the life of prayer, and the proportion in which they come to each soul differs.

So too the spiritual lands into which prayer brings us has its mountains, oceans, and plains so rich and great that no one person can explore them appropriately. Still less can anyone live in all of it. We are each to practice prayer according to what God shows us, and we can do that, but we cannot forget the overplus of experience which is not for us but for other souls. As those in quiet inland places may still remember the great movement of the sea, we must try to avoid insularity. It may seem to us that we've been set down, as it were, to grub spiritual potatoes, but from somewhere else they might be seen as very special flowers.

Amid all the varieties of prayer there are two movements which must, I think, be present in every spiritual life. The love and energy of prayer must be directed on the one hand toward God and on the other toward humanity. In the first movement we turn toward the Supernatural, to God in Himself. In the second movement, we turn with added energy toward the Natural. Prayer, like the whole of human inner life, swings between the unseen and the seen. Both movements are necessary, but the second will only be well done when the first has the central place. Here *lex credendi* is or should be *lex orandi.* In other words, "what we believe" would be "what we pray." That old Latin saying is, of course, in the reverse order: *Lex orandi; lex credendi,* and that means that our belief (and therefore its expression in action) come from our prayer.

Furthermore, "Thou shalt love the Lord thy God" comes *first* (not only in the Commandments, and not only in action, but in prayer). This means that adoration, and not intercession or petition, is the very heart of the life of prayer.

Prayer is a supernatural achievement (made possible by God within us) and must be directed to a supernatural end. It must begin, end, and be enclosed in the atmosphere of adoration. It must aim at God, for and in Himself. It too must acknowledge the soul's basic law: "We come from God. We belong to God. We tend toward God."

Perhaps some of us have prayed in the words or spirit of William Law: "May all within me be changed into Thy Holy Spirit and temper." But unless we give time to look at, love, and lose ourselves in contemplation of our path, it is not very likely that prayer will be effective.

Fussy, anxious, exclusively practical, this-world prayer does nothing to enrich Christian character. The reason is quite plain. Prayer is substantially communion with God, and therefore exclusive attention to Him is its first part. We must receive before we can transmit. Our effect as transmitters of His grace and love directly depends on our adoring attention. His spirit is always with us. In the prayer of love, attention, and adoration, we open our doors wide to receive Him. We abase ourselves and acknowledge our nothingness in comparison with his wonder, perfection, and joy. The Soul that has given itself to God becomes part of that Mystical Body in and through which He acts on life. Its destiny is to be a receiver and transmitter of grace.

Is that not practical work? For Christians, is it not the *only* practical work?

But sometimes we are in such a hurry to transmit that we forget that the primary need is to receive in order to nourish our adoring love, our sense of awe, our personal littleness and dependence. Doing this, perpetually turning to Him, adoring Him, losing ourselves in Him, our souls are slowly flooded by His Spirit. Only when our own souls are thus filled to the brim can we presume to offer spiritual gifts to others. When we *are* filled, we shan't be able to help giving.

St. Bernard reminds us that people who are reservoirs are not meant to be canals. The remedy for that sense of impotence, that desperate spiritual exhaustion which religious workers, functioning only as canals, too often know, is an inner life governed not by petition, but by adoring prayer. This is Christ's message and attitude. The very heart of His prayer and doctrine is the presence, the love, the glory of God everywhere awaiting our recognition, knowing our needs before we ask. Christ said little about petition, because he was penetrated by the love and generosity of God.

When we find that demands on us are threats to our inward poise, when we feel signs of starvation and stress, it is time to call a halt and redirect our balance. Then it is imperative to reestablish the fundamental relationship of our souls with Eternal Reality, the home and Father of our spirits. Our hearts shall have no rest save there.

It is only when our hearts are thus at rest in God in peaceful, selfless adoration that we can show His attractiveness to others. In the flood tide of such adoring prayer the soul is carried up to God, is hidden in God. Thus alone can it achieve that utter self-forgetfulness which is the basis of its peace and power. But peace and power can never be ours as long as we make our prayer a means of drawing gifts to ourselves from God instead of an act of self-giving to Him.

From this adoring prayer, this steady concentration on God and joyous self-immolation before Him, springs all other prayerful disposition in our souls. A deep, humble, contrite sense of our unworthiness, gratitude for all that has been given us, learning an increased charity that longs to spend itself on other souls—all these are signs of spiritual vitality, and spiritual vitality depends on the *feeding* of our souls on God. Without that, we can't expect to be strong enough to work for Him.

The full Christian life of prayer swings to and fro between adoration and action. We must be sure that the outward swing toward God is full, generous, unhurried, brimming with joy. Many of us live exacting lives of service full of hard material problems. If we can acquire the determination that *nothing* shall turn us from a steady daily habit of loving adoration, our prayer will be full of loving intimacy and awe. Then we shall have the best of all helps for the maintenance of the soul's energy and peace, and we will serve God with a quiet mind.

This adoring prayer of loving communion with God may take many forms. The point is, we must find the form that suits *us*—*our* souls—*yours*, not someone else's. Now, at this state of growth, we cannot conceive our prayer in ape fashion. We must not try to imitate that which someone else has told us. Some, who by looking at Christ, meditate on His words and acts, come close to His Spirit and lose themselves in loving worship, entering into ever closer union with Him. Some find in the sacramental life the heart of prayer. Some feel most deeply drawn to self-abasement before the spaceless presence of God. We can't all feel *all* these things.

Our prayer too will change as our souls mature. We must never attempt uniformity. Our task is to act simply, to speak or keep silent as we are impelled. There are little phrases of love and worship, fragments from the Psalms, which often help us to keep our mind pointing in the right way and open up the way for some who find this prayer difficult at first. Think of St. Francis repeating all night: "My God and All!" The perfect prayer of adoration is the humble cry of awed delight. The creature gazes on the Creator and Lord.

Don't all examples and tiresome details fall away and vanish as we dwell on such words? Don't they bring us back to trust that the important thing in prayer is never what we say or ask for, but the way we feel about God?—our attitude?

Complete, loving surrender. You may think that I've insisted unduly on this. It is because I feel that here in current religious life there is a great neglect of humble duty and humble joy. It is this which is responsible for much lack of spiritual depth and power. Adoration, however, is the central service asked by God of human souls. I often think that those who by health, age, and circumstance withdraw from active life, may be so withdrawn (for nothing happens by chance) in order that they may add to the world's gift of adoration—the true music of the spheres.

And isn't this especially true of *sufferers?* We have all seen the peaceful, joyous suffering which witnesses to God—which seems, as it were, to live within Christ and to sing for Christ—just as Francis did! Over against that, what a waste is fretful, melancholic suffering, the suffering that *isn't* prayer, that makes suffering sub-human. Whereas pain, transmuted by adoring love, makes the sufferer superhuman—in a phrase of the mystics, "a partaker of the Divine Nature"—so too, in *our* ordained vocation of prayer and work, the transmuting effect is what counts.

We may not have time for long prayers, though we should make a great effort to set apart *some* regular period of exclusive attention to God. But we *can* form a habit of making short acts of love, adoration, and resignation at odd moments. An important part of education in prayer is to recall us to the atmosphere of Eternity. If we feel slack, dry, or spiritually listless, and all do at times, there is no better way of tuning ourselves up than by deliberately making such acts as these. Such habits will produce a state of mind in which we best use our longer periods of prayer and best maintain the deep serenity of the Child of God through the perpetual strain of pressing practical life.

This deep, self-oblivious, persistent serenity is not those special feelings we may have when praise is the real test of the worth and purity of our prayer. Some people never have those feelings, and it's a great reassurance to them to know that they don't matter. St. Teresa reminds us in formidable language that what *does* matter is *never* our special devotional experiences, but always their results: the fruits of prayer.

The Fruits of the Spirit are love, joy, peace, patience, long-suffering, gentleness, goodness, and faith: "the mind that was in Christ." If, in our adoration, we have truly and selflessly poured ourselves out to the Spirit and opened up our souls, that is the temper which will come to dominate our lives: a sweet and humble spirit of acceptance which turns all it touches into gold by bringing it within the radius of God.

So wonderful tonight—as if one were plunged in that Ocean of Love—swallowed up—breathless with a sort of formless joy—all edges gone and yet it is distinct. So enraptured, it's hardly adoration, and in it, deep wordless communion with the Spirit of Jesus—the two sides together like that. Three-fourths of an hour. No words for it. Worried about mother, the Baron, everything: but it didn't matter—nothing *there* but deep, inexplicable joy and peace. Almost intolerable in one way and yet so heavenly and so safe. Couldn't think or make acts or see anything clearly. It was like the Mirror (of Simple Souls) says, "She *feels* no joy, for she herself *is* joy"— all far too great and strong for one to grasp.

APRIL 13, 1924

Tremendous ups and downs lately. All too dazed holding on light sensations during and after mother's death—inability to *feel* all the things people were attributing to me. Lost my prayer for a time, everything seeming to be resting on me. Went through all with a sort of iron steadiness. Necessary to make absolute acts of acceptance in all that may be in God's will—even giving our home up if it turns out needful—with determination to let *nothing* break my life of prayer. At first very distracted and on the rocks, but it has come back now with several spells of quietude, just kneeling at the feet of Christ quite close and in silence. Today, such clear sense of being as it were a *cell* in a boundless living web through which redeeming work can be done and so closely linked with the others . . . sharing and exchanging strength and prayer— being one's self but never alone now. I think this is a bit of what St. Paul was feeling when he spoke of the Mystical Body. These New Testament sayings are so much deeper and more realistic than clergymen think. Somehow at the darkest moments, reading à Kempis, saw entirely new meaning in the Cross and *how* little I know of it really, and what mysterious deeps there are waiting for me there.

EASTER, 1924

Have such a distinct consciousness from time to time of now being actually educated by God. And what I've got, largely, to do is to let it happen. Makes the light and dark fluctuations, etc., comparatively unimportant. When hindered in prayer, etc., no need to fuss: but rather accept this and all other difficulties gratefully as very useful mortifications licking me into shape for His purposes. I don't matter in the very *least*— this gets more and more obvious if only one could remember it—and the further this certitude goes the calmer and happier I am.

OCTOBER 16, 1924

This morning in prayer suddenly I was compelled to say: Take all my powers from me rather than ever let me use them again for my own advantage. When I'd said it, some strange and quite unseizable movement happened in my soul—I knew I had made a real vow, a more crucial act of dedication than ever before and shall be taken at my word. There was a darkening, deepening, and enlargement, a sort of "melting into the supreme."

I see only too clearly that the only possible end of this road is complete, unconditional self-consecration, and for this I have not the nerve, the character or the depth. There has been some sort of mistake. My soul is too small for it and yet it is at the bottom the only thing that I really want. It feels sometimes as if, while still a jumble of conflicting impulses and violent faults, I were being pushed from behind towards an edge I *dare not* jump over.

understanding mysticism

1925-1931

Mystics of the Church

In Mystics of the Church, *Evelyn Underhill affirms profound spirituality as a natural and historic aspect of Christianity. Rather than something alien and threatening, mysticism has always had a vital role in the life of the Church.*

From *Mystics of the Church*

Ecstatic phenomena were almost taken for granted in the Early Church; and St. Paul's distinction as a mystic lies not in their possession, but in the detachment with which he regarded them. Thus in AD 52, when he wrote his first letter to the Corinthians, he acknowledged his continued possession of the much-prized "gift of tongues"; those outbursts of ecstatic but unintelligible speech common in times of religious excitement. But his attitude toward such external "manifestations of the Spirit" is marked by a cool common sense which must amaze us when we consider the period in which he wrote, the universal respect for the marvelous, and the circumstances of his own conversion. His rule is simple. He discounts any "gifts" and experiences which do not help other souls. The mystical communion of his soul with Christ must not be a matter of personal enjoyment; it must support and not supplant the apostolic career. "Forasmuch as ye are zealous of spiritual gifts, seek that ye may excel to the upbuilding of the Church. . . . I will pray with the Spirit, *and* I will pray with the understanding too."

Personal Journal

1926

FROM "GREEN AND FLOWERED NOTEBOOKS"

NOTES MADE IN RETREAT, MAY 1926

In all things where free choice is offered me, my use or renunciation of things and conditions must be governed by the question whether they are favorable or inimical to my service of God. This will *include* their direct effect on my soul's life; and more besides.

I must desire and elect only such things as best contribute to this final end of a life of adoration and service. Of each choice offered me, I must ask: how does this help, how does this hinder, the one aim? Apart from this consideration I must be indifferent to pain/pleasure, success/failure, and so forth. First quality required: absolute and equable Patience.

My own improvement and my ultimate state, my work in other souls, and which souls I shall help; all this shall never be self-chosen, but entirely determined by God. "Our activity spoils all, when it precedes the divine action instead of following it."

My own place in the spiritual universe, though minute, is yet unique. The work that I have to do and can do is my own, and no one else's. *This* work, in *this* place, can satisfy God and procure my sanctification, if done with purity and generosity and without self-love. If it fails to effect this, the fault is *mine*.

It is *essential* that I do full justice to the ordinary domestic bits of my life, as equally given me by God with the rest. These are direct instruments of mortification to all my worst passions: impatience, pride, self-will, uncharitableness, egotism, claimfulness. Must respond to *all* the people He puts in my life, so far as I can—not limit sympathy to the ones I like. Work out on the material He provides—the central principles of love, sympathy, abnegation, and forgiveness.

Since my faults, and the difficulties which keep me back most, are those connected with social and domestic contacts, the humble fulfillment of all duties on this side of life, steady effort at gentleness, pliability, and self-forgetfulness, uncritical affection and sympathy, *immediate* ascetic aim.

I am as much required to be a Christian wife-daughter-mistress-friend, as to be a writer on religion and director of souls. Must combat persistent self-occupation by forcing myself to enter into interest of others, however alien from my own.

All distinct failures in love: harshness, moroseness, intolerance, resentfulness, uncharitableness; to be punished by first available humiliating or distasteful act; remember I have *no* rights, status, or claim on consideration.

God in this Retreat has given me a clear view of my faults, and also of my call to His absolute service. It is *imperative* that I undertake the serious and painful purification of my unmortified nature hour by hour and day by day, and allow myself *no* quarter, *no* excuses under the needs of health, nerves, and temperament.

I see that it *is* possible to become such that Christ can act in and through one in utter peace and steadiness: O that this should be the final aim set before my soul, the *raison d'être* of all practices and mortifications, and the object of the sacramental life.

Concerning the Inner Life

This is a little volume of three informal talks "delivered at a school for clergy in the North of England, and . . . published at the request of some of those who heard them."

From *Concerning the Inner Life*

Who then are real people of prayer? They are those who deliberately will and steadily desire that their intercourse with God and other souls shall be controlled and actuated at every point by God Himself; those who have so far developed and educated their spiritual sense, that their supernatural environment is more real and solid to them than their natural environment. Men and women of prayer are not necessarily those who say a number of offices, or abound in detailed intercessions, but they are children of God, who are and know themselves to be in the depths of their souls attached to God, and are wholly and entirely guided by the Creative Spirit in their prayer and their work. This is not merely a bit of pious language. It is a description, as real and concrete as I can make it, of the only really apostolic life. Every Christian starts with a chance of it; but only a few develop it. The laity distinguish in a moment the clergy who have it from the clergy who have it not: there is nothing that you can do for God or for the souls of men, which exceeds in importance the achievement of that spiritual temper and attitude.

By contemplative prayer, I do not mean any abnormal sort of activity or experience, still less a deliberate and artificial passivity. I just mean the sort of prayer that aims at God in and for Himself and not for any of His gifts whatever, and more and more profoundly rests in Him alone: what St. Paul, that vivid realist, meant by being *rooted* and *grounded*. When I read those words, I always think of a forest tree. First of the bright and changeful tuft that shows itself to the world, and produces the immense spread of boughs and branches, the succession and abundance of leaves and fruits. Then of the vast unseen system of roots, perhaps greater than the branches in strength and extent, with their tenacious attachments, their fan-like system of delicate filaments and their power of silently absorbing food. On that profound and secret life the whole growth and stability of the tree depend. It is rooted and grounded in a hidden world.

That was the image in Paul's mind, I suppose, when he talked of this as the one prayer he made for his converts and fellow workers; and said that he desired it for them so that they could "be able to comprehend what is the breadth and length and depth and height"—a splendor of realization unachieved by theology—and be "filled with all the fullness of God": in other words, draw their spiritual energy direct from its supernatural source. You know that St. Bernard called this the "business of all businesses"; because it controls all the rest, and gives meaning to all the rest—perpetually renews our contact with reality. Ought not our devotional life to be such as to frame in us the habit of such recourse to God as the Ground of the soul? Should it not educate our whole mental machinery, feeling, imagination, will, and thought, for this?

We have the saints to show us that these things are actually possible: that one human soul can rescue and

transfigure another, and can endure for it redemptive
hardship and pain. We may allow that the saints are specialists;
but they are specialists in a career to which all Christians are
called. They have achieved, as it were, the classic status.
They are the advance guard of the army; but we, after all, are
marching in the main ranks. The whole army is dedicated to
the same supernatural cause; and we ought to envisage it as a
whole, and to remember that every one of us wears the same
uniform as the saints, has access to the same privileges, is
taught the same drill and fed with the same food. The difference
between them and us is a difference in degree, not in kind.
They possess, and we most conspicuously lack, a certain
maturity and depth of soul caused by the perfect flowering in
them of self-oblivious love, joy, and peace. We recognize in
them a finished product, a genuine work of God. But this
power and beauty of the saints is on the human side simply
the result of their faithful life of prayer, and is something to
which, in various degrees, every Christian worker can attain.
Therefore we ought all to be a little bit like them, to have a
sort of family likeness, to share the family point of view.

If we ask of the saints how they achieved spiritual
effectiveness, they are only able to reply that, in so far as
they did it themselves, they did it by love and prayer: a love
that is very humble and homely; a prayer that is full of adoration
and of confidence. Love and prayer, on their lips, are not
mere nice words; they are the names of tremendous powers,
able to transform in a literal sense human personality and
make it more and more that which it is meant to be—the
agent of the Holy Spirit in the world. Plainly then, it is
essential to give time or to get time somehow for self-training
in this love and this prayer, in order to develop those powers.
It is true that in their essence they are "given," but the gift is
only fully made our own by a patient and generous effort of
the soul. Spiritual achievement costs much, though never as

much as it is worth. It means at the very least the painful development and persevering, steady exercise of a faculty that most of us have allowed to get slack. It means an inward if not an outward asceticism: a virtual if not an actual mysticism.

People talk about mysticism as if it were something quite separate from practical religion, whereas, as a matter of fact, it is the intense heart of all practical religion, and no one without some touch of it is contagious and able to win souls. What *is* mysticism? It is in its widest sense the reaching out of the soul to contact with those eternal realities which are the subject matter of religion. And the mystical life is the complete life of love and prayer which transmutes those objects of belief into living realities: love and prayer directed to God for God Himself, and not for any gain for ourselves.

☙

We shall find, when we look into our own souls, or study those with whom we have to deal, that there is an immense variation among them, both in aptitude, and in method of approaching God. We shall discover that only certain devotional books and certain devotional symbols and practices truly have meaning for us, whilst others will appeal to other people. Some of us belong predominantly to the institutional, some to the ascetical and ethical, some to the mystical type; and within these great classes and types of spirituality, there is an infinite variety of temper and degree. The first thing we have to find out is the kind of practice that suits *our* souls— ours, not someone else's, and now, at this stage of its growth. You have to find and develop the prayer that fully employs you and yet does not overstrain you; the prayer in which you are quite supple before God; the prayer that refreshes, braces, and expands you, and is best able to carry you over the inevitable fluctuations of spiritual level and mood. But in thus making up your minds to use that method towards which you are most deeply and persistently attracted, and to feed your own souls on the food that you can digest, you must nevertheless retain an entire and supple willingness to give others, if desirable, a quite different diet, encourage in them another sort of practice. More than this, you must for their sakes try to learn all you can about methods other than your own.

☙

It seems to me that there are four main things which must have a place in any full and healthy religious life, and that a remembrance of this will help us to make our own inner lives balanced and sane. We require, first, the means of gaining and holding a right attitude; secondly, right spiritual food—real, nourishing food with a bite in it, not desiccated and predigested piety. "*I* am the food of the full grown," said the voice of God to St. Augustine; "grow and feed on *Me.*" Thirdly, we need an education which will help growth, training our spiritual powers to an ever greater expansion and efficiency. Fourthly, we have or ought to have some definite spiritual work, and must see that we fit ourselves to do it.

Now each of these four needs is met by a different type of prayer. The right attitude of the soul to God is secured and supported by the prayer of pure adoration. The necessary food for its growth is obtained through our spiritual reading and meditation, as well as by more direct forms of communion. Such meditation will also form an important stage in the education of the spiritual faculties; which are further trained in some degree by the use of such formal, affective, or recollective prayer as each one of us is able to employ. Finally, the work which can be done by the praying soul covers the whole field of intercession and redemptive self-oblation.

Take first then, as primary, the achievement and maintenance of a right attitude towards God: that profound and awe-struck sense of His transcendent reality, that humbly

adoring relation, on which all else depends. I feel no doubt
that, for all who take the spiritual life seriously—and above
all for the minister of religion—this prayer of adoration
exceeds all other types in educative and purifying power. It
alone is able to consolidate our sense of the supernatural, to
conquer our persistent self-occupation, to expand our spirits,
to feed and quicken our awareness of the wonder and the
delightfulness of God. There are two movements which must
be plainly present in every complete spiritual life. The energy
of its prayer must be directed on the one hand towards God,
and on the other towards people. The first movement
embraces the whole range of spiritual communion between
the soul and God: in it we turn towards Divine Reality in
adoration, bathing, so to speak, our souls in the Eternal Light.
In the second we return, with the added peace and energy
thus gained, to the natural world, there to do spiritual work
for and with God for other men. Thus prayer, like the whole
of man's inner life, "swings between the unseen and the seen."
Now both these movements are of course necessary in all
Christians, but the point is that the second will only be well
done where the first has the central place. The deepening of
the soul's unseen attachments must precede, in order that it
may safeguard the outward swing towards the world.

This means that adoration, and not intercession or
petition, must be the very heart of the life of prayer. For
prayer is a supernatural activity or nothing at all, and it must
primarily be directed to supernatural ends. It too acknowledges
the soul's basic law: it comes from God, belongs to God, is
destined for God. It must begin, end, and be enclosed in the
atmosphere of adoration; aiming at God for and in Himself.
Our ultimate effect as transmitters of the supernal light and
love directly depends on this adoring attentiveness. In such a
prayer of adoring attentiveness, we open our doors wide to
receive His ever-present Spirit; abasing ourselves and

acknowledging our own nothingness. Only the soul that has thus given itself to God becomes part of the mystical body through which He acts on life. Its destiny is to be the receiver and transmitter of grace.

Is not that practical work? For Christians, surely, the only practical work. But sometimes we are in such a hurry to transmit that we forget our primary duty is to receive, and that God's self-imparting through us will be in direct proportion to our adoring love and humble receptiveness. Only when our souls are filled to the brim can we presume to offer spiritual gifts to other people. The remedy for that sense of impotence, that desperate spiritual exhaustion which religious workers too often know, is, I am sure, an inner life governed not by petition but by adoring prayer. When we find that the demands made upon us are seriously threatening our inward poise, when we feel symptoms of starvation and stress, we can be quite sure that it is time to call a halt, to re-establish the fundamental relation of our souls with Eternal Reality, the Home and Father of our spirits. "Our hearts shall have *no* rest save in Thee." It is only when our hearts are thus actually at rest in God, in peaceful and self-oblivious adoration, that we can hope to show His attractiveness to other people.

In the flood tide of such adoring prayer, the soul is released from the strife and confusions of temporal life; it is lifted far beyond all petty controversies, petty worries, and petty vanities—and none of us escape these things. It is carried into God, hidden in Him. This is the only way in which it can achieve that utter self-forgetfulness which is the basis of its peace and power, and which can never be ours as long as we make our prayer primarily a means of drawing gifts to ourselves and others from God, instead of an act of unmeasured self-giving. I am certain that we gradually and imperceptibly learn more about God by this persistent attitude of humble adoration, than we can hope to do by any amount of mental exploration. For in it our soul recaptures, if only for a moment, the fundamental relation of the tiny created spirit with its Eternal Source, and the time is well spent which is spent in getting this relation and keeping it right. In it we breathe deeply the atmosphere of Eternity; and when we do that, humility and common sense are found to be the same thing. We realize, and re-realize, our tininess, our nothingness, and the greatness and steadfastness of God. And we all know how priceless such a realization is, for those who have to face the grave spiritual risk of presuming to teach others about Him.

Moreover, from this adoring prayer and the joyous self-immolation that goes with it, all the other prayerful dispositions of our souls seem, ultimately, to spring. A deep, humble contrition, a sense of our creaturely imperfection and unworthiness, gratitude for all that is given us, burning and increasing charity that longs to spend itself on other souls— all these things are signs of spiritual vitality: and spiritual vitality depends on the loving adherence of our spirits to God. Thus it is surely of the first importance for those who are called to exacting lives of service, to determine that nothing shall interfere with the development and steady daily practice of loving and adoring prayer: a prayer full of intimacy and awe. It alone maintains the soul's energy and peace, and checks the temptation to leave God for His service. I think that if you have only as little as half an hour to give each morning to your private prayer, it is not too much to make up your minds to spend half that time in such adoration. For it is the central service asked by God of human souls, and its neglect is responsible for much lack of spiritual depth and power. Moreover, it is more deeply refreshing, pacifying, and assuring than any other type of prayer. "Unlike, much unlike," says à Kempis, "is the savor of the creator and the creature, of everlastingness and of time, of light uncreated and light illuminate." But only those know this who are practiced in adoring love.

You may reasonably say: This is all very well, and on general religious grounds we shall all agree about the beauty and desirability of such prayer. But how shall we train ourselves, so persistently called away and distracted by a multitude of external duties, to that steadfastly theocentric attitude? This brings us to the consideration of the further elements necessary to the full maintenance of the devotional life—its food and its education. If we want to develop this power of communion, to correspond with the grace that invites us to it, we must nourish our souls carefully and regularly with such noble thoughts of God as we are able to assimilate, and we must train our fluctuating attention and feeling to be obedient to the demands of the dedicated will. We must become, and keep, spiritually fit.

We shall, of course, tend to do this feeding and this training in many different ways. No one soul can hope to assimilate all that is offered to us by the richness of Reality. Thus some temperaments are most deeply drawn to adoration by a quiet dwelling upon the spaceless and changeless Presence of God; some, by looking at Christ, or by meditating in a simple way on His acts and words, as recorded in the Gospels, lose themselves in loving communion with Him. Some learn adoration best through the sacramental life. We cannot all feel all these things in their fullness; our spiritual span is not wide enough for that. Therefore we ought to practice humbly and with simplicity those forms of reflective meditation and mental prayer that help us most; and to which, in times of tranquility, we find ourselves most steadily drawn. We grow by feeding, not by forcing; and should be content in the main to nourish ourselves on the food that we can digest and quietly leave the other kinds for those to whom they appeal. In doing this, however, we shall be wise if we do not wholly neglect even those types of spirituality which attract us least. Thus the natural prayer of the philosophic soul, strongly drawn by the concept of Eternal and Infinite Spirit, becomes too thin, abstract, and inhuman if it fails to balance this by some dwelling on the historic and revealed, some sacramental integration of spirit and of sense; the born contemplative drifts into quietism without the discipline of vocal or liturgical prayer; while Christocentric devotion loses depth and awe unless the object of its worship is seen within the horizon of Eternity. Therefore it is well to keep in mind some sense of the rich totality out of which our little souls are being fed.

There is, however, one kind of prayer which all these differing types and levels of spirituality can use and make their own, and which is unequalled in psychological and religious effectiveness. This is the so-called "prayer of aspirations": the frequent and attentive use of little phrases of love and worship, which help us, as it were, to keep our minds pointing the right way, and never lose their power of forming and maintaining in us an adoring temper of soul. The Psalms, the Confessions of St. Augustine, the Imitation of Christ, are full of such aspiratory prayers, which range from the most personal to the most impersonal conceptions of God, and are fitted to every mood and need. They stretch and re-stretch our spiritual muscles, and, even in the stuffiest surroundings, can make us take deep breaths of mountain air. The habit of aspiration is difficult to form, but once acquired exerts a growing influence over the soul's life. Think of St. Francis of Assisi repeating all night: "My God and All! What art Thou? And what am I?" Is not that a perfect prayer of adoration? The humble cry of the awed and delighted creature, gazing at its Creator and Lord. Think of the exclamation of the Psalmist: "Whom have I in heaven but Thee? And what is there on earth that I desire beside Thee?" Do not all the tangles and tiresome details fall away and vanish when we dwell on such words? And do they not bring us back to the truth, that the most important thing in prayer is never what we say or ask for, but our *attitude* towards God? What it all comes to is this: that the personal religion of the priest must be theocentric. It must conform to the rule laid down by the great Bérulle: that one's true relation to God consists solely in adoration and adherence, and that these two moods or attitudes of soul cover the whole range of one's inner life and must be evoked and expressed by prayer.

The question of the proper feeding of our own devotional life must, of course, include the rightful use of spiritual reading. And with spiritual reading we may include formal or informal meditation upon Scripture or religious truth: the brooding consideration, the savoring—as it were the chewing of the cud—in which we digest that which we have absorbed, and apply it to our own needs. Spiritual reading is, or at least it can be, second only to prayer as a developer and support of the inner life. In it we have access to all the hoarded supernatural treasure of the race: all that it has found out about God. It should not be confined to Scripture, but should also include at least the lives and the writings of the canonized and uncanonized saints: for in religion variety of nourishment is far better than a dyspeptic or fastidious monotony of diet. If we do it properly, such reading is a truly social act. It gives to us not only information, but communion: real intercourse with the great souls of the past, who are the pride and glory of the Christian family. Studying their lives and work, slowly and with sympathy; reading the family history, the family letters; trying to grasp the family point of view, we gradually discover these people to be in origin though not in achievement very much like ourselves. They are people who are devoted to the same service, handicapped often by the very same difficulties; and yet whose victories and insights humble and convict us, and who can tell us more and more, as we learn to love more and more, of the relation of the soul to Reality. The Confessions of St. Augustine, the Dialogue of St. Catherine of Siena, Tauler's Sermons, Gerlac Petersen's "Fiery Soliloquy with God," the Revelations of Julian of Norwich, the Life of St. Teresa, the little book of Brother Lawrence, the Journals of Fox, Woolman, and Wesley—the meditative, gentle, receptive reading of this sort of literature immensely enlarges our social and spiritual environment. It is one of the ways in which the communion of saints can be most directly felt by us.

We all know what a help it is to live among, and be intimate with, keen Christians, how much we owe in our own lives to contact with them, and how hard it is to struggle on alone in a preponderantly non-Christian atmosphere. In the saints we always have the bracing society of keen Christians. We are always in touch with the classic standard. Their personal influence still radiates, centuries after they have left the earth, reminding us of the infinite variety of ways in which the Spirit of God acts on people through people, and reminding us too of our own awful personal responsibility in this matter. The saints are the great experimental Christians, who, because of their unreserved self-dedication, have made the great discoveries about God; and, as we read their lives and works, they will impart to us just so much of these discoveries as we are able to bear. Indeed, as we grow more and more, the saints tell us more and more, disclosing at each fresh reading secrets that we did not suspect. Their books are the work of specialists, from whom we can humbly learn more of God and of our own souls.

≒

Meditation not only feeds, it also disciplines the mind and soul, gradually training us to steady our attention upon spiritual things, an art especially difficult to those beset by many responsibilities and duties. It helps us to conquer distractions, and forms with most of us an essential prelude to that state of profound recollection in which the soul dwells almost without effort on the things of God. It is generally and rightly regarded as one of the principal elements in an ordered devotional life. Most people, I suppose, who have taken the trouble to learn it, get their spiritual food very largely by this deliberate exercise of brooding, loving thought: entering into, dwelling on, exploring, and personally applying the deeds and the words of Christ or of the saints, or the fundamental conceptions of religion. . . .

There are people, however, who find that they simply cannot practice these formal and discursive meditations: the effort to do so merely stultifies itself. Where this inability is genuine, and not a disguised laziness, it generally coexists with a strong attraction to a more simple and formless communion with God: that loving and generalized attention which is sometimes called "simple regard" or "affective prayer," and has been beautifully described as "the prayer which articulates nothing but expresses everything: specifies nothing and includes everything." I think those in whom this tendency is marked and persistent should yield to it, abandon their own efforts, and move with docility towards that form of communion to which they feel drawn, remembering that anything we may achieve in the world of prayer only represents our particular way of actualizing one tiny fragment of the supernatural possibilities offered to the race, and that any attempt to reduce the soul's intercourse with the Transcendent to a single system or formula is condemned in advance.

The obstinate pursuit of a special state of meditation or recollection always defeats itself, bringing into operation the law of reversed effort, and concentrating attention on the struggle to meditate instead of on its supernatural end. Yet it is not uncommon to find people forcing themselves from a mistaken sense of duty to develop or continue a devotional method which was never appropriate to their nature, or which they have now outgrown. They deliberately thwart a genuine though as yet unformed attraction to silent communion by struggling hard to perform a daily formal meditation, because they have made this a part of their rule of life; or they desperately get through a routine of intercessions and vocal prayers to which they have been injudiciously bound, and which now limit the freedom of their access to God. On the other hand, persons whose natural expression is verbal, and who need the support of concrete image, make violent efforts to "go into the silence" because some wretched little book has told them to do so. True silent prayer is full of power and beauty; but I suppose few things are more stultifying in effect than this deliberate and artificial passivity. It is not by such devices that we feed the soul; their only result must be spiritual indigestion.

❧

I want to say something about a factor which is always present in every developed life of prayer: the liability to spiritual dryness and blankness, painful to all fervent Christians, but specially distressing to those whose business it is to work with souls. The times when all your interest and sense of reality evaporate, when the language of religion becomes meaningless and you are quite unable, in any real sense, to pray. Everyone is so off-color from time to time; and it is one of the great problems of the priest and religious teacher, to know how, under these conditions, he can best serve God and other souls. Now first of all, it is possible to reduce the intensity of such desolations—to use the technical term—by wise handling of yourselves; and here prudent self-treatment is plainly your duty—the dictates of grace and common sense coincide. The condition is largely psychological. It is a fatigue state, a reaction sometimes from excessive devotional fervor, sometimes from exacting spiritual work, which has exhausted the inner reserves of the soul. It almost always follows on any period of marked spiritual progress or enlightenment. In either case, the first point is, accept the situation quietly. Don't aggravate it, don't worry, don't dwell on it, don't have contrition about it; but turn, so far as you can, to some secular interest or recreation and *"wait till the clouds roll by."* Many a priest ends every Sunday in the state of exhaustion in which he cannot possibly say his own prayers, in which, as one of them observed, the only gift of the Spirit in which he is able to take any interest is a hot bath. That is a toll levied by his psycho-physical limitations. Effort and resistance will only make it worse.

But it is a toll that can be turned into a sacrifice. It is one of the most painful obligations of the life of the religious worker, that he is often called upon to help other souls when he is in desolation himself. He has got to put a good face on it—to listen to their raptures or their despairs—to give himself without stint in serving—never to betray anything of his own inner state. And this is one of the most purifying of all experiences that can come to him; for it contains absolutely no food for self-satisfaction, but throws him completely back upon God. I think it is above all in work done in times of aridity and desolation that the devotional life of the priest shows its worth.

Correspondence

1927

Baron von Hügel's death created a vacancy for other spiritual directors in Evelyn's life. While now a competent and much desired spiritual director herself, she still sought guidance. Walter Frere, Bishop of Truro, became von Hügel's successor.

LETTER TO BISHOP FRERE

My dear Director,

You were kind enough to say that I might write when I wanted to, and the result of the leisure of the holidays is that there are one or two points I would very much like to put before you. Very likely they are not worth your attention. In that case of course I shan't expect any answer and anyhow it is only a case of feeling easier if I have your authority just to go on or make a change.

This is in the nature of a confession. Since your last letter I really have tried to avoid hovering over faults, etc. But sometimes things jump out at one. And I've been horrified lately to find I've slipped into a wickedness against which I really *did* think I was on my guard—self-will and love of power in direction work. In a queer way things happen, within two days four of my usually docile children resisted or acted against my advice in various ways, or preferred the guidance of others—and this, when on my own firmly held principles

I *ought* to have accepted quite calmly, as a matter of fact I minded very much indeed. I really am ashamed to tell you this but must—because if self-will and self-love have got in *here*, it's fatal, isn't it? Nothing could be worse and some really severe measures must be taken.

The other point is a good deal more intimate, and if I hadn't been to _____ I don't think I should have ventured to speak about it. But after that I knew you would understand and not think it awful. Until about five years ago I had never had any personal experience of our Lord: I didn't know what it meant. I was a convinced theocentric, thought most Christocentric language and practice sentimental and super- stitious and was very handy with shallow psychological explanations of it. I had from time to time what seemed to be vivid experiences of God, from the time of my conversion from agnosticism (about twenty years ago now). This position I thought to be that of a broad-minded and intelligent Christian, but when after a severe spiritual smash and partial recovery, I went to the Baron, he said I wasn't much better than a Unitarian! Somehow by his prayers or something he *compelled* me to experience Christ. He never said anything more about it—but I know humanly speaking he did it. It took about four months—it was like watching the sun rise very slowly—and then suddenly one knew what it was.

Now for sometime after this I remained predominately theocentric. But for the last two or three years and specially lately, more and more my whole religious life and experience seems centered with increasing vividness on our Lord—that sort of quasi-involuntary prayer which springs up of itself at odd moments is always now directed to Him. I seem to have to try as it were to live more and more towards Him only— it's all this which makes it so utterly heartbreaking when one is horrid. The New Testament, which once I couldn't make much of, or meditate on, now seems full of things never noticed—all gets more and *more* alive and compelling and beautiful. Sometimes the sense of His Presence is so vivid, I wonder what will happen next. And then of course come flat times when I wonder on the contrary if it was all a dream. Holy Communion, which at first I did simply under obedience, gets more and more wonderful too. It's in that world and atmosphere one lives. Now I feel rather uneasy about all this for:

I know how fatally easy it is to slide into religious sentimentalism and make devotion into an emotional satisfaction of a quite unspiritual kind, and that "consolations" have a very dangerous side. And I've a *perfect* horror of all that sort of thing. Yet this is all so calm and heavenly when it happens and so infinitely beyond oneself, and of course there are plenty of dull and distracted times when one can only "carry on." Perhaps it's only a Calvinistic twist that makes one suspicious of yielding to such entrancing happiness, and one ought to accept and be thankful. But in spite of the reassuring things the books say, I do feel a sort of scruple about it.

The Baron used to say that a well-balanced religion required the theocentric *and* incarnational sides together: that no one got this quite right and most fervent people were Christocentric to excess and let their rightful devotion to our Lord swamp their sense of God Himself, and the fact that not *even* Christ exhausted the richness and possibility of God. He thought my danger was in the opposite direction, but I don't know what he would think now. Yet after all, St. Paul goes a long way in the Christocentric direction, and it's the sort of things he says, not all the horrible remarks of the Song of Solomon-ish school of pietists, that now seem so actual and so realistic.

The increased concentration makes it so much more difficult than before to meet on their own ground the people who have arrived at a sort of all-overish theism and feel

"Hindus are often nearer God than Christians," and that there are "other ways to Him" and so forth. Certainly I do believe that He does reveal Himself in many ways to those in good faith. But more and more I do feel the *absolute* difference of real Christianity, and it's this that these people won't admit. At bottom Christ is to them an idea, not a living fact, and that creates a barrier. It's the conviction of His factualness that I'm powerless to give them—it doesn't depend of course on argument—and anyhow I simply *can't* speak about it. When they bring out all the stuff about Christ being a world teacher, or the parallels of the Mystery religions, the high quality of Buddhist ethics, etc., I just feel what shallow, boring, unreal twaddle it is! But feeling that doesn't win souls for God—and it would be perfectly ghastly if one let oneself turn a Pious Person comfortably ensconced in one's own prayers and with only one prescription to offer, wouldn't it?

This next winter I've had to say I'll do *no* lecturing, retreat work, etc.—a disgusting concession to mere health which ought to be paid for somehow. So would it be all right, without making a rigid rule (for which I feel less and less need and inclination), to spend rather more time, when I can, in prayer and informal meditation? At present I am running my old rule of one and a half hours daily mostly in a very informal and take-it-as-it-comes sort of way. In my mixed and much interrupted life *exact* fixed times aren't possible.

Journal

1927

NOTES MADE IN RETREAT, JULY 1927

1. I am asked for an absolute humble, ungrudging forgiveness, to be renewed if necessary; recognizing that I am partly, even largely, to blame for what has happened and that my past faults and sins were patiently borne with, and my (at least virtual) disloyalties accepted. Also I must definitely exert myself to be more gentle, genial, and companionable, and to provide the relief and variety one needs and ought to get through home life. Mortify my own preference for quiet, carefully develop mutual interests, make up for any sacrifice made. And all this not out of prudence but out of charity; because it is part of the response asked by God.

2. I see that the sacramental life is and must be one with the crucified life. It is association with our Lord's whole sacrifice and incomplete without a share in the Cross. Must regard all suffering sent by God as an opportunity of this. The Eucharist marks the first station on the Way of the Cross.

3. If I could serve, humbly, generously, and lovingly, those who have in any way injured me, how great this would be.

4. Far more care and detailed love and devotion to the poor, and all the souls God sends me, without regard to personal preference.

5. Stern mortification of acquisitive and possessive instincts—spend on others, give to others, demand and expect *nothing*. Abandon all claimfulness and grudging attitudes. Have a secret fear of discomfort and poverty, which must go. *Choose* poverty and neglect.

6. Carefully distinguish the two elements in my nature—steadily fight lower, natural, self-interested self—quietly and carefully feed spiritual self. "Self-love, self-will, and self-interest" still rampant in my soul even where disguised. Poverty of spirit is the only way out, with quiet letting-go of *all* rights and possessions and general support of rights and possessions of others. Not be distressed or afraid when things are taken from me: regard it as an honor.

7. Must more and more put the wine of religion into the water of common life; and try to appear less absorbed in purely religious interests, pick up and develop natural interests; especially those of other people.

8. More grateful recollection of all that has been given me: in love, friendship (e.g., Wilfred's devotion), saintly influences—the Bishop, Gwen, Rosa, etc.—utterly undeserved opportunities for work for God and encouraging results. Glad acceptance of failures, criticism, snubs, sense of isolation, when *those* come.

9. When people don't understand me, not to assume they are stupid or in the wrong.

10. Definite call to wide and generous spending of love—remember am minister of love, or *nothing*. Impossible to love *enough*. Especially try to include those to whom I'm not naturally attracted and who may be craving for love I ought to give: not the *à deux* kind [mutual love] but the entirely undemanding kind—the *gift*. Only if I give myself can I ever be consecrated.

11. Try to be more strict about my rule.

12. Am definitely committed to be a *disciple of our Lord*—

be taught by Him, try to follow Him—and only as *this* does He give Himself to me sacramentally, as one under discipline. Totally submitted, learning in following, and at all costs including the Cross.

13. Realize I am a *very* slow learner and have only got on a few inches yet, and my best experiences are nothing at all against what others have. In this retreat I have been given finally a new and deeper state of prayer, very interior and still, as if one was poured down within oneself to an utterly hushed, unmoving place where one can remain, without apparent succession, before Christ. Perhaps this is the "ground," bare and silent.

14. Read the foregoing once a month till next retreat.

Essay

THE HOUSE OF THE SOUL

When St. Paul described our mysterious human nature as a "temple of the Holy Spirit"—a created dwelling-place or sanctuary of the uncreated and invisible divine life—he was stating in the strongest possible terms a view of our status, our relation to God, which has always been present in Christianity and is indeed implicit in the Christian view of reality. But that statement as it stands seems far too strong for most of us. We do not feel in the very least like the temples of creative love. We are more at ease with St. Teresa, when she describes the soul as an "interior castle"—a roomy mansion, with various floors and apartments from the basement upwards, not all devoted to exalted uses, not always in a satisfactory state. And when, in a more homely mood, she speaks of her own spiritual life as "becoming solid like a house," we at last get something we can grasp.

The soul's house, that interior dwelling-place which we all possess, for the upkeep of which we are responsible—a place in which we can meet God, or from which in a sense we can exclude God—that is not too big an idea for us. Though no imagery drawn from the life of sense can ever be adequate to the strange and delicate contacts, tensions, demands, and benedictions of the life that lies beyond sense; though the important part of every parable is that which it fails to express; still, here is a conception which can be made to cover many of the truths that govern the interior life of prayer.

First, we are led to consider the position of the house. However interesting and important its peculiarities may seem to the tenant, it is not as a matter of fact an unusually picturesque and interesting mansion made to an original design and set in its own grounds with no other building in sight. Christian spirituality knows nothing of this sort of individualism. It insists that we do not inhabit detached residences but are parts of a vast spiritual organism, that even the most hidden life is never lived for itself alone. Our soul's house forms part of the vast City of God. Though it may not be an important mansion with a frontage on the main street, nevertheless it shares all the obligations and advantages belonging to the city as a whole. It gets its water from the main, and its light from the general supply. The way we maintain and use it must have reference to our civic responsibilities.

It is true that God creates souls in a marvelous liberty and variety. The ideals of the building estate tell us nothing about the Kingdom of Heaven. It is true, also, that the furnishing of our rooms and cultivation of our garden is largely left to our personal industry and good taste. Still, in a general way, we must fall in with the city's plan and consider, when we hang some new and startling curtains, how they will look from the street. However intense the personal life of each soul may be, that personal life has got out of proportion if it makes us forget our municipal obligations and advantages; for our true significance is more than personal, it is bound up with the fact of our status as members of a supernatural society. So into all the affairs of the little house there should enter a certain sense of the city, and beyond this of the infinite world in which the city stands: some awestruck memory of our double situation, at once so homely and so mysterious. We must each maintain unimpaired our unique relation with God, yet without forgetting our intimate contact with the rest of the city, or the mesh of invisible life which binds all the inhabitants in one.

For it is on the unchanging life of God, as on a rock, that the whole city is founded. That august and cherishing Spirit is the atmosphere which bathes it, and fills each room of every little house—quickening, feeding, and sustaining. He is the one reality which makes us real, and, equally, the other houses too. "If I am not in Thee," said St. Augustine, "then I am not at all." We are often urged to think of the spiritual life as a personal adventure, a ceaseless hustle forward, with all its meaning condensed in the "perfection" of the last stage. But though progress, or rather growth, is truly in it, such growth in so far as it is real can only arise from, and be conditioned by, a far more fundamental relation—the growing soul's abidingness in God.

Next, what type of house does the soul live in? It is a two-storey house. The psychologist too often assumes that it is a one-roomed cottage with a mud floor, and never even attempts to go upstairs. The extreme transcendentalist sometimes talks as though it were perched in the air, like the lake dwellings of our primitive ancestors, and had no ground floor at all. A more humble attention to facts suggests that neither of these simplifications is true. We know that we have a ground floor, a natural life biologically conditioned, with animal instincts and affinities, and that this life is very important, for it is the product of the divine creativity—its builder and maker is God. But we know too that we have an upper floor, a supernatural life with supernatural possibilities, a capacity for God, and that this, the peculiar prerogative of human beings, is more important still. If we try to live on one floor alone we destroy the mysterious beauty of our human vocation, so utterly a part of the fugitive and creaturely life of this planet and yet so deeply colored by eternity, so entirely

one with the world of nature and yet, "in the Spirit," a habitation
of God. "Thou madest him lower than the angels, to crown
him with glory and worship." We are created both in time
and in eternity, not truly one but truly two; and every
thought, word and act must be subdued to the dignity of
that double situation in which Almighty God has placed and
companions the childish spirit of humanity.

Therefore a full and wholesome spiritual life can never
consist in living upstairs and forgetting to consider the
ground floor and its homely uses and needs, thus ignoring the
humbling fact that those upper rooms are entirely supported
by it. Nor does it consist in the constant, exasperated
investigation of the shortcomings of the basement. When St.
Teresa said that her prayer had become "solid like a house,"
she meant that its foundations now went down into the lowly
but firm ground of human nature, the concrete actualities of
the natural life, and on those solid foundations its wall rose
up towards heaven. The strength of the house consisted in
that intimate welding together of the divine and the human
which she found in its perfection in the humanity of
Christ. There, in the common stuff of human life which He
blessed by His presence, the saints have ever seen the
homely foundations of holiness. Since we are two-storey
creatures, called to a natural and a supernatural status, both
sense and spirit must be rightly maintained, kept in order,
consecrated to the purposes of the city, if our full obligations
are to be fulfilled. The house is built for God, to reflect, on
each level, something of His unlimited Perfection.
Downstairs, that general rightness of adjustment to all this-
world obligations, which the ancients called the quality of
justice, and the homely virtues of prudence, temperance, and
fortitude reminding us of our creatureliness, our limitations,
and so humbling and disciplining us. Upstairs, the heavenly
powers of faith, hope, and charity, tending towards the

eternal, nourishing our life towards God, and having no meaning apart from God.

But the soul's house will never be a real home unless the ground floor is as cared for and as habitable as the beautiful rooms upstairs. We are required to live in the whole of our premises, and are responsible for the condition of the whole of our premises. It is useless to repaper the drawing-room if what we really need is a new sink. In that secret divine purpose which is drawing all life towards perfection, the whole house is meant to be beautiful, and ought to be beautiful, for it comes from God and was made to His design. Christ's soul when on earth lived in one of these houses, had to use the same fitments, make the same arrangements do. We cannot excuse our own failures by attributing them to the inconvenience of the premises, and the fact that some very old-fashioned bits of apparatus survive. Most of us have inherited some ugly bits of furniture, or unfortunate family portraits which we can't get rid of, and which prevent our rooms being quite a success. Nevertheless the soul does not grow strong merely by enjoying its upstairs privileges and ignoring downstairs disadvantages, problems, and responsibilities, but only by tackling its real task of total transformation. It is called to maintain a house which shall be in its completeness "a habitation of God in the Spirit," subdued to His purpose on all levels, manifesting His glory in what we call natural life as well as in what we call spiritual life. For humanity is the link between these two orders: truly created a little lower than the angels, yet truly crowned with glory and worship, because in this unperfected human nature the Absolute Life itself has deigned to dwell.

That means, reduced to practice, that the whole house with its manifold and graded activities must be a house of prayer. It does not mean keeping a Quiet Room to which we can retreat, with mystical pictures on the walls and curtains over the windows to temper the disconcerting intensity of the light, a room where we can forget the fact that there are black beetles in the kitchen, and that the range is not working very well. Once we admit any violent contrast between the upper and lower floor, the "instinctive" and "spiritual" life, or feel a reluctance to investigate the humbling realities of the basement, our life becomes less, not more, than human and our position is unsafe. Are we capable of the adventure of courage which inspires the great prayer of St. Augustine: "The house of my soul is narrow; do Thou enter in and enlarge it! It is ruinous; do Thou repair it"? Can we risk the visitation of the mysterious power that will go through all our untidy rooms, showing up their shortcomings and their possibilities, reproving by the tranquility of order the waste and muddle of our inner life? The mere hoarded rubbish that ought to go into the dustbin, the things that want mending and washing, the possessions we have never taken the trouble to use? Yet this is the only condition on which human beings can participate in that fullness of life for which they are made.

The Lord's Prayer, in which St. Teresa said that she found the whole art of contemplation from its simple beginning to its transcendent goal, witnesses with a wonderful beauty and completeness to this two-storey character of the soul's house, and yet its absolute unity. It begins at the top, in the watch-tower of faith, with the sublime assertion of our supernatural status—the one relation, intimate yet inconceivable, that governs all the rest—"Our Father who art in Heaven, hallowed be *Thy* name." Whatever the downstairs muddle and tension we have to deal with, however great the difficulty of adjusting the claims of the instincts that live in the basement and the interests that clamor at the door, all these demands, all this rich and testing experience is enfolded and transfused by the cherishing, overruling life and power of God. We are lifted clear of the psychological tangle in which the life of our spirit too often seems enmeshed, into the pure, serene light of eternity, and shown the whole various and disconcerting pageant of creation as proceeding from God and existing only that it may glorify His name. Childlike dependence and joyful adoration are placed together as the twin characters of the soul's relation to God.

Thence, step by step, this prayer brings us downstairs, goes with us through the whole house, bringing the supernatural into the natural, blessing and sanctifying, cleansing and rectifying every aspect of the home. "*Thy* Kingdom come!" Hope—trustful expectation. "*Thy* will be done!" Charity—the loving union of our wills with the Infinite Will. Then the ground floor. "Give us this day"—that food from beyond ourselves which nourishes and sustains our life. Forgive all our little failures and excesses, neutralize the corroding power of our conflicts, disharmonies, rebellions, sins. We can't deal with them alone. Teach us, as towards our fellow citizens, to share that generous tolerance of God. Lead us not into situations where we are tried beyond our strength, but meet us on the battlefield of personality, and protect the weakness of the adolescent spirit against the downward pull of the inhabitants of the lower floor.

And then, the reason of all this, bringing together, in one supreme declaration of joy and confidence, the soul's sense of that supporting, holy, and eternal Reality who is the Ruler and the Light of the city, and of every room in every little house. *Thine* is the Kingdom, the power, and the glory. If our interior life be subdued to the spirit of this prayer, with its rich sense of our mighty heritage and childlike status, our total dependence on the reality of God, then the soul's house is truly running well. Its action is transfused by contemplation. The door is open between the upper and the lower floors, the life of spirit and the life of sense.

"Two cities," said St. Augustine, "have been created by two loves: the earthly city by love of self even to contempt of God, the heavenly city by love of God even to contempt of self. The one city glories in itself; the other city glories in the Lord. The one city glories in its own strength; the other city says to its God, "I will love Thee, O Lord my strength." Perhaps there has never been a time in Christian history when that contrast has been more sharply felt than it is now—the contrast between that view of the human situation and meaning in which the emphasis falls on humanity, its vast desires and wonderful achievements, even to contempt of God, and the view in which the emphasis falls on God's transcendent action and overruling will, even to contempt of self. St. Augustine saw, and still would see, humanity ever at work building those two cities, and every human soul as a potential citizen of one or the other. And from this point of view, that which we call the "interior life" is just the home life of those who inhabit the invisible City of God, realistically taking up their municipal privileges and duties and pursuing them "even to contempt of self." It is the obligation and the art of keeping the premises entrusted to us in good order, having ever in view the welfare of the city as a whole.

Some souls, like some people, can be slummy anywhere. There is always a raucous and uncontrolled voice ascending from the basement, and a pail of dirty water at the foot of the stairs. Others can achieve in the most impossible situation a simple and beautiful life. The good citizen must be able without reluctance to open the door at all times, not only at the weekend; must keep the windows clean and taps running properly, that the light and living water may come in. These free gifts of the supernatural are offered to each house, and only as free gifts can they be had. Our noisy little engine will not produce the true light, nor our most desperate digging a proper water supply. Recognition of this fact, this entire dependence of the creature, is essential if the full benefits of our mysterious citizenship are ever to be enjoyed by us. "I saw," said the poet of the Apocalypse, "the holy city coming *down* from God out of heaven . . . the glory of God lit it . . . the water of life proceeded out of the throne of God." All is the free gift of the supernatural, not the result of human growth and effort. God's generous and life-giving work in the world of souls ever goes before humanity's work in God. So the main thing about the Invisible City is not the industry and good character of the inhabitants; they do not make it shine. It is the tranquil operation of that perpetual providence which incites and supports their small activities; the direct and childlike relation in which they stand to the city's Ruler; the generous light and air that bathe the little houses; the unchanging rock of eternity on which their foundations stand.

mature insight

1932-1941

Personal Journal and Correspondence

1933

FRUIT OF RETREAT

A whole and complete self-offering to God for His unseen purpose, willing to accept suffering, darkness, struggle, temptation at His good pleasure.

A promise that wherever I go I will say Peace and try to bring Peace.

That I will give my own spiritual life without reserve into the keeping of God and strive to make my interior attitude one of weak adoration before God.

That I will seek to rejoice in the progress of others, especially those who overpass me, rejecting all movements of envy and spiritual jealousy, trying to take lowest place.

That I will be silent about my own interior sufferings and try to offer them to God.

1934

LETTERS TO MARGARET CROPPER

It looks as if I should do that Christian Worship book— rather exciting. R. S. W. strongly approves if they give me two or three years for it. . . . I've definitely accepted the Christian Worship Book, and now feel frightened and incompetent. . . . I've taken a very fierce decision. I'm going to have a complete year off from retreats in 1935, except one at Pleshey Ascensiontide for my regular "children" and retreatants, with meditation and directed prayers but no addresses. I think this ought to be nice—and a sort of feeling I've had lately that I just must make a break (this is my 11th year of them)—was brought to a head by Lucy and Marjorie Vernon writing to me quite independently to say that it had come to them so strongly that I ought to have a year off and devote myself to the Worship book, that they felt forced to tell me. So I referred the matter to R. S. W. who said he was quite clear I ought, from every point of view. I only hope everyone won't think I've become an R. C., or had a mental breakdown!!!

The Spiritual Life

1936

Evelyn delivered three radio addresses on the BBC. These intimate talks were published together in a volume bearing the title The Spiritual Life.

FROM THE SPIRITUAL LIFE

"The Spiritual Life" is a dangerously ambiguous term; indeed, it would be interesting to know what meaning any one reader at the present moment is giving to these three words. Many, I am afraid, would really be found to mean "the life of my own inside": and a further section to mean something very holy, difficult, and peculiar—a sort of honors course in personal religion—to which they did not intend to aspire.

Both these kinds of individualist—the people who think of the spiritual life as something which is for themselves and about themselves, and the people who regard it as something which is not for themselves—seem to need a larger horizon, within which these interesting personal facts can be placed, and seen in rather truer proportion. Any spiritual view which focuses attention on ourselves, and puts the human creature with its small ideas and adventures in the center foreground, is dangerous till we recognize its absurdity. So at least we will try to get away from these petty notions, and make a determined effort to see our situation within that great spiritual landscape which is so much too great for our limited minds to grasp, and yet is our true inheritance—a present reality here and now, within which our real lives are now being lived. We will look at it through the wide-angle lens of disinterested worship, and put aside those useful little spectacles which bring into sharp focus our own qualities, desires, interest, and difficulties, but blur everything else.

There it is, in its splendor and perfection, "shining to saints in a perpetual bright clearness," as Thomas à Kempis said. Not only the subject matter of religion, but also the cause and goal of everything in human life that points beyond the world—great action, great music, great poetry, great art. Our attention to it, or our neglect of it, makes no difference to that world; but it makes every difference to us. For our lives are not real, not complete, until they are based on a certain conscious correspondence with it: until they become that which they are meant to be—tools and channels of the Will of God—and are included in the Kingdom of Spirits which live in, to, and for Him alone.

Christians, of course, acknowledge that Will and that Kingdom as the greatest of all realities every time they say the Lord's Prayer—that is, if they really grasp its tremendous implications, and really mean what they say. But so many Christians are like deaf people at a concert. They study the program carefully, believe every statement made in it, speak respectfully of the quality of the music, but only really hear a phrase now and again. So they have no notion at all of the mighty symphony which fills the universe, to which our lives are destined to make their tiny contribution, and which is the self-expression of the Eternal God.

Yet there are plenty of things in our normal experience, which imply the existence of that world, that music, that life. If, for instance, we consider the fact of prayer, the almost universal impulse to seek and appeal to a power beyond ourselves, and notice the heights to which it can rise in those who give themselves to it with courage and love—the power it exerts, the heroic vocations and costly sacrifices which it supports, the transformations of character which it effects— it is a sufficiently mysterious characteristic of man. Again and again it is discredited by our popular rationalisms and naturalisms, and again and again it returns and claims its rights within human life, even in its crudest, most naïve expressions retaining a certain life-changing power. No one who studies with sympathy, for instance, the history of religious revivals, can doubt that here, often in a grotesque and unlovely disguise, a force from beyond the world really breaks in upon the temporal order with disconcerting power.

So, too, all who are sensitive to beauty know the almost agonizing sense of revelation its sudden impact brings—the abrupt disclosure of the mountain summit, the wild cherry-tree in blossom, the crowning moment of a great concerto, witnessing to another beauty beyond sense. And again, any mature person looking back on their own past life, will be forced to recognize factors in that life, which cannot be attributed to heredity, environment, opportunity, personal initiative, or mere chance. The contact which proved decisive, the path unexpectedly opened, the other path closed, the thing we felt compelled to say, the letter we felt compelled to write. It is as if a hidden directive power, personal, living, free, were working through circumstances and often against our intention or desire, pressing us in a certain direction, and molding us to a certain design.

All this, of course, is quite inexplicable from the materialistic standpoint. If it is true, it implies that beneath the surface of life, which generally contents us, there are unsuspected deeps and great spiritual forces which condition and control our small lives. Some people are, or become, sensitive to the pressure of these forces. The rest of us easily ignore the evidence for this whole realm of experience, just because it is all so hidden and interior, and we are so busy responding to obvious and outward things. But no psychology which fails to take account of it can claim to be complete. When we take it seriously, it surely suggests that we are essentially spiritual as well as natural creatures; and that therefore life in its fullness, the life which shall develop and use all our capacities and fulfill all our possibilities, must involve correspondence not only with our visible and ever-changing, but also with our invisible and unchanging environment: the Spirit of all spirits, God, in whom we live and move and have our being. The significance, the greatness of humanity, consists in our ability to do this. The meaning of our life is bound up with the meaning of the universe. Even though so far the consciousness of this ability and this meaning is latent in the mass of men; yet what an enhancement of life, what devotedness, heroism, and capacity for suffering and for love, what a sure hold upon reality it already produces in those who have felt its attraction, and who respond with courage and without reserve to its demands.

When we consider our situation like that, when we lift our eyes from the crowded by-pass to the eternal hills, then, how much the personal and practical things we have to deal with are enriched. What meaning and coherence come into our scattered lives. We mostly spend those lives conjugating three verbs: to Want, to Have, and to Do. Craving, clutching, and fussing, on the material, political, social, emotional, intellectual—even on the religious—plane, we are kept in perpetual unrest: forgetting that none of these verbs have any ultimate significance, except so far as they are transcended by and included in, the fundamental verb, to Be: and that Being, not wanting, having, and doing, is the essence of a spiritual life. But now, with this widening of the horizon, our personal ups and downs, desires, cravings, efforts, are seen in scale as small and transitory spiritual facts, within a vast, abiding spiritual world, and lit by a steady spiritual light. And at once a new coherence comes into our existence, a new tranquility and release. Like a chalet in the Alps, that homely existence gains atmosphere, dignity, significance from the greatness of the sky above it and the background of the everlasting hills.

The people of our time are helpless, distracted, and rebellious, unable to interpret that which is happening, and full of apprehension about that which is to come, largely because they have lost this sure hold on the eternal which gives to each life meaning and direction, and with meaning and direction gives steadiness. I do not mean by this a mere escape from our problems and dangers, a slinking away from the actual to enjoy the eternal. I mean an acceptance and living out of the actual, in its homeliest details and its utmost demands, in the light of the eternal, and with that peculiar sense of ultimate security which only a hold on the eternal brings. When the vivid reality which is meant by these rather abstract words is truly possessed by us, when that which is unchanging in ourselves is given its chance, and emerges from the stream of succession to recognize its true home and goal, which is God—then, though much suffering may, indeed will remain, apprehension, confusion, instability, despair, will cease.

This, of course, is what religion is about: this adherence to God, this confident dependence on that which is unchanging. This is the more abundant life, which in its own particular language and own particular way, it calls us to live. Because it is our part in the one life of the whole universe of spirits, our share in the great drive towards Reality, the tendency of all life to seek God, Who made it for Himself, and now incites and guides it, we are already adapted to it, just as a fish is adapted to live in the sea. This view of our situation fills us with a certain awed and humble gladness. It delivers us from all niggling fuss about ourselves, prevents us from feeling self-important about our own little spiritual adventures, and yet makes them worth while as part of one great spiritual adventure.

It means, when we come down again to our own particular case, that my spiritual life is not something specialized and intense: a fenced-off devotional patch rather difficult to cultivate, and needing to be sheltered from the cold winds of the outer world. Nor is it an alternative to my outward, practical life. On the contrary, it is the very source of that quality and purpose which makes my practical life worthwhile. The practical life of a vast number of people is not, as a matter of fact, worth while at all. It is like an impressive fur coat with no one inside it. One sees many of these coats occupying positions of great responsibility. Hans Andersen's story of the king with no clothes told one bitter and common truth about human nature; but the story of the clothes with no king describes a situation just as common and even more pitiable.

Still less does the spiritual life mean a mere cultivation of one's own soul, poking about our interior premises with a flashlight. Even though in its earlier stages it may, and generally does, involve dealing with ourselves, and that in a drastic way, and therefore requires personal effort and personal choice, it is also intensely social; for it is a life that is shared with all other spirits, whether in the body or out of the body, to adopt St. Paul's words. You remember how Dante says that directly a soul ceases to say Mine, and says Ours, it makes the transition from the narrow, constricted, individual life to the truly free, truly personal, truly creative spiritual life, in which all are linked together in one single response to the Father of all spirits, God. Here, all interpenetrate, and all, however humble and obscure their lives may seem, can and do affect each other. Every advance made by one is made for all.

Only when we recognize all this and act on it, are we fully alive and taking our proper place in the universe of spirits;

for life means the fullest possible give and take between the living creature and its environment: breathing, feeding, growing, changing. And spiritual life, which is profoundly organic, means the give and take, the willed correspondence of the little human spirit with the Infinite Spirit, here where it is: its feeding upon Him, its growth towards perfect union with Him, its response to His attraction and subtle pressure. That growth and that response may seem to us like a movement, a journey, in which by various unexpected and often unattractive paths, we are drawn almost in spite of ourselves—not as a result of our own over-anxious struggles—to the real end of our being, the place where we are ordained to be: a journey which is more like the inevitable movement of the iron filing to the great magnet that attracts it, than like the long and weary pilgrimage in the teeth of many obstacles from "this world to that which is to come." Or it may seem like a growth from the childlike, half-real existence into which we are born into a full reality.

There are countless ways in which this may happen, sometimes under conditions which seem to the world like the very frustration of life, of progress, of growth. Thus boundless initiative is chained to a sick bed and transmuted into sacrifice, the lover of beauty is sent to serve in the slum, the lover of stillness is kept on the run all day, the sudden demand to leave all comes to the one who least expects it, and through and in these apparent frustrations the life of the spirit emerges and grows. So those who imagine that they are called to contemplation, because they are attracted by contemplation, when the common duties of existence steadily block this path, do well to realize that our own feelings and preferences are very poor guides when it comes to the robust realities and stern demands of the Spirit.

St. Paul did not want to be an apostle to the Gentiles. He wanted to be a clever and appreciated young Jewish scholar, and kicked against the pricks. St. Ambrose and St. Augustine did not want to be overworked and worried bishops. Nothing was farther from their intention. St. Cuthbert wanted the solitude and freedom of his hermitage on the Farne; but he did not often get there. St. Francis Xavier's preference was for an ordered life close to his beloved master, St. Ignatius. At a few hours' notice he was sent out to be the Apostle of the Indies and never returned to Europe again. Henry Martyn, the fragile and exquisite scholar, was compelled to sacrifice the intellectual life to which he was so perfectly fitted for the missionary life to which he felt he was decisively called. In all these, a power beyond themselves decided the direction of life. Yet in all we recognize not frustration, but the highest of all types of achievement. Things like this—and they are constantly happening—gradually convince us that the over-ruling reality of life is the Will and Choice of a Spirit acting not in a mechanical but in a living and personal way, and that the spiritual life of man does not consist in mere individual betterment, or assiduous attention to his own soul, but in a free and unconditional response to that Spirit's pressure and call, whatever the cost may be.

The first question here, then, is not "What is best for my soul?" nor is it even "What is most useful to humanity?" But—transcending both these limited aims—"What function must this life fulfill in the great and secret economy of God?" How directly and fully that principle admits us into the glorious liberty of the children of God, where we move with such ease and suppleness, because the whole is greater than any of its parts and in that whole we have forgotten ourselves.

Indeed, if God is All and His Word to us is All, that must mean that He is the reality and controlling factor of every situation, religious or secular, and that it is only for His glory and creative purpose that it exists. Therefore our favorite distinction between the spiritual life and the practical life is false. We cannot divide them. One affects the other all the time: for we are creatures of sense and of spirit, and must live an amphibious life. Christ's whole Ministry was an exhibition, first in one way and then in another, of this mysterious truth. It is through all the circumstances of existence, inward and outward, not only those which we like to label spiritual, that we are pressed to our right position and given our supernatural food. For a spiritual life is simply a life in which all that we do comes from the center, where we are anchored in God: a life soaked through and through by a sense of His reality and claim, and self-given to the great movement of His will.

Most of our conflicts and difficulties come from trying to deal with the spiritual and practical aspects of our life separately instead of realizing them as parts of one whole. If our practical life is centered on our own interest, cluttered up by possessions, distracted by ambitions, passions, wants, and worries, beset by a sense of our own rights and importance, or anxieties for our own future, or longings for our own success, we need not expect that our spiritual life will be a contrast to all this. The soul's house is not built on such a convenient plan: there are few soundproof partitions in it. Only when the conviction—not merely the idea—that the demand of the Spirit, however inconvenient, comes first and IS first, rules the whole of it, will those objectionable noises die down which have a way of penetrating into the nicely furnished little oratory, and drowning all the quieter voices by their din.

St. John of the Cross, in a famous and beautiful poem, described the beginning of the journey of his soul to God:

"In an obscure night
Fevered by Love's anxiety
O hapless, happy plight
I went, none seeing me,
Forth from my house, where all things quiet be"

Not many of us could say that. Yet there is no real occasion for tumult, strain, conflict, anxiety, once we have reached the living conviction that God is All. All takes place within Him. He alone matters, He alone is. Our spiritual life is His affair; because, whatever we may think to the contrary, it is really produced by His steady attraction, and our humble and self-forgetful response to it. It consists in being drawn, at His pace and in His way, to the place where He wants us to be, not the place we fancied for ourselves.

Some people may seem to us to go to God by an escalator, where they can assist matters a bit by their own efforts, but much gets done for them and progress does not cease. Some appear to be whisked past us in an elevator; whilst we find ourselves on a steep flight of stairs with a bend at the top, so that we cannot see how much farther we have to go. But none of this really matters; what matters is the conviction that all are moving towards God, and, in that journey, accompanied, supported, checked, and fed by God. Since our dependence on Him is absolute, and our desire is that His Will shall be done, this great desire can gradually swallow up, neutralize all our small self-centered desires. When that happens life, inner and outer, becomes one single, various act of adoration and self-giving, one undivided response of the creature to the demand and pressure of Creative Love.

There are certain questions and difficulties which turn up again and again in relation to the spiritual life. Of these, one of the most fundamental concerns the Nature of God, and the way in which men should think of Him, and in particular, whether Christians can properly use the word Reality and other terms of an impersonal and philosophic sort as synonyms for God. I think that they can and should do so. In religion, where familiar words so easily lose their full meaning for us, it is often valuable to use other words which, though they cannot indeed express the full truth, emphasize other aspects of our great spiritual inheritance. St. Augustine surely answers this question when he says, "God is the only Reality, and we are only real in so far as we are in His order and He in us." St. Augustine was a great Christian. Nothing could exceed the fervor of his personal communion with God. Yet it is the impersonal revelation of a Power and Beauty "never new, yet never old," which evokes his greatest outbursts of adoring joy. The truth is we must use both personal and impersonal language if our fragmentary knowledge of the richness of God's Being is to be expressed; and a reminder of this fact is often a help to those for whom the personal language of religion has become conventional and unreal.

This leads to the next question of importance, which also involves our view of the Nature of God. When we consider the evil, injustice, and misery existing in the world, how can we claim that the ultimate Reality at the heart of the universe is a Spirit of peace, harmony, and infinite love? What evidence can we bring to support such a belief? And how can we adore a God whose creation is marred by cruelty, suffering, and sin?

This is, of course, the problem of evil, the crucial problem for all realistic religion. It is no use to dodge this issue, and still less use to pretend that the Church has a solution of the problem up her sleeve. I would rather say with Baron von Hügel that Christian spirituality does not explain evil and suffering, which remain a mystery beyond the reach of the human mind, but does show us how to deal with them. It insists that something has gone wrong, and badly wrong, with the world. That world as we know it does not look like the work of the loving Father whom the Gospels call us to worship, but rather, like the work of selfish and undisciplined children who have been given wonderful material and a measure of freedom, and not used that freedom well. Yet we see in this muddled world a constant struggle for Truth, Goodness, Perfection; and all those who give themselves to that struggle—the struggle for the redemption of the world from greed, cruelty, injustice, selfish desire, and their results—find themselves supported and reinforced by a spiritual power which enhances life, strengthens will, and purifies character. And they come to recognize more and more in that power the action of God. These facts are as real as the other facts, which distress and puzzle us: the apparent cruelty, injustice, and futility of life. We have to account somehow for the existence of gentleness, purity, self-sacrifice, holiness, love; and how can we account for them, unless they are attributes of Reality? Christianity shows us in the most august of all examples the violence of the clash between evil and the Holiness of God. It insists that the redemption of the world, defeating the evil that has infected it by the health-giving power of love—bringing in the Kingdom of God—is a spiritual task, in which we are all required to play a part. Once we realize this, we can accept—even though we cannot understand—the paradox that the world as we know it contains much that is evil, and yet, that its Creator is the one supreme Source and Object of the love that will triumph in the end.

Such a view of our vocation as this brings with it another fundamental question. How are we to know, or find out, what the Will of God is? I do not think that any general answer can be given to this. In clear moral and political issues, we must surely judge and act by the great truths and demands of Christianity; and if we have the courage to do this, then, as we act, more and more we shall perceive the direction of the Will. That choice, cause, or action, which is least tainted by self-interest, which makes for the increase of happiness— health—beauty—peace—cleanses and harmonizes life, must always be in accordance with the Will of the Spirit which is drawing life towards perfection. The difficulty comes when there is a conflict of loyalties, or a choice between two apparent gods. At such points many people feel unaware of any guidance, unable to discern or understand the signals of God; not because the signals are not given, but because the mind is too troubled, clouded, and hurried to receive them. "He who is in a hurry," said St. Vincent de Paul, "delays the things of God." But when those who are at least attempting to live the life of the Spirit, and have consequently become more or less sensitive to its movements, are confronted by perplexing choices, and seem to themselves to have no clear light, they will often become aware, if they will wait in quietness, of a subtle yet insistent pressure in favor of the path which they should take. The early Friends were accustomed to trust implicitly in indications of this kind, and were usually justified. Where there is no such pressure, then our conduct should be decided by charity and common sense, qualities which are given to us by God in order that they may be used.

Next, we are obliged to face the question as to how the demand of modern psychology for complete self-expression, as the condition of a full and healthy personal life, can be reconciled with the discipline, choice, and sacrifice which are essential to a spiritual life; and with this the allegation made by many psychologists that the special experiences of such a spiritual life may be dismissed as disguised wish-fulfillments. In the first place, the complete expression of everything of which we are capable—the whole psychological zoo living within us, as well as the embryonic beginnings of artist, statesman, or saint—means chaos, not character. We must select in order to achieve; we can only develop some faculties at the expense of others. This is just as true for the man of action or of science as it is for the man of religion. But where this discipline is consciously accepted for a purpose greater than ourselves, it will result in a far greater strength and harmony, a far more real personality, than the policy of so-called self-expression. As to the attempt to discredit the spiritual life as a form of wish-fulfillment, this has to meet the plain fact that the real life of the Spirit has little to do with emotional enjoyments, even of the loftiest kind. Indeed, it offers few attractions to the natural man, nor does it set out to satisfy his personal desires. The career to which it calls him is one that he would seldom have chosen for himself. It proceeds by way of much discipline and renunciation, often of many sufferings, to a total abandonment to God's purpose which leaves no opening even for the most subtle expressions of self-love.

I come now to the many people who, greatly desiring the life of communion with God, find no opportunity for attention to Him in an existence which often lacks privacy, and is conditioned by ceaseless household duties, exacting professional responsibilities, or long hours of work. The great spiritual teachers, who are not nearly so aloof from normal life as those who do not read them suppose, have often dealt with this situation, which is not new, though it seems to press with peculiar weight upon ourselves. They all make the same answer: that what is asked of us is not necessarily a great deal of time devoted to what we regard as spiritual things, but the constant offering of our wills to God, so that the practical duties which fill most of our days can become part of His order and be given spiritual worth. So Père Grou, whose writings are among the best and most practical guides to the spiritual life that we possess, says, "We are always praying, when we are doing our duty and turning it into work for God." He adds that among the things which we should regard as spiritual in this sense are our household or professional work, the social duties of our station, friendly visits, kind actions, and small courtesies, and also necessary recreation of body and of mind, so long as we link all these by intention with God and the great movement of His Will.

So those who wonder where they are to begin, might begin here, by trying to give spiritual quality to every detail of their everyday lives, whether those lives are filled with a constant succession of home duties, or form part of the great systems of organized industry or public service, or are devoted to intellectual or artistic ends. . . .

It is this constant correlation between inward and outward that really matters; and this has always been the difficulty for human beings, because there are two natures in us, pulling different ways, and their reconciliation is a long and arduous task. Many people seem to think that the spiritual life necessarily requires a definite and exacting plan of study. It does not. But it does require a definite plan of life, and courage in sticking to the plan, not merely for days or weeks, but for years. New mental and emotional habits must be formed, all our interests re-arranged in new proportion round a new center. This is something that cannot be hurried; but, unless we take it seriously, can be infinitely delayed. Many people suggest by their behavior that God is of far less importance than their bath, morning paper, or early cup of tea. The life of co-operation with Him must begin with a full and practical acceptance of the truth that God alone matters, and that He, the Perfect, always desires perfection. Then it will inevitably press us to begin working for perfection: first in our own characters and actions, next in our homes, surroundings, profession, and country. We must be prepared for the fact that even on small and personal levels this will cost a good deal, frequently thwarting our own inclinations and demanding real sacrifice.

Personal Note

1936

NOTES FOR REGINALD SOMERSET WARD, OCTOBER 1936

Am not in the least reluctant to draw in and give up expressive work, but so far don't make anything of it. If God really *means* me for a water pipe, putting the cork in will throw things out of gear. At first I felt sure—now I feel unsure. Don't get any prayer done. Feel reluctant to do retreats but this may be just the effort. Have lost interest in this sort of work, but that doesn't prove I oughtn't to do it!

Worship

Underhill's "other big book" is Worship. *She was quite feeble when she wrote it, but it demonstrates a mind and spirit that remained vital. It was her last major effort.*

From *Worship*

Worship, in all its grades and kinds, is the response of the creature to the Eternal: nor need we limit this definition to the human sphere. There is a sense in which we may think of the whole life of the Universe, seen and unseen, conscious and unconscious, as an act of worship, glorifying its Origin, Sustainer, and End. Only in some such context, indeed, can we begin to understand the mergence and growth of the spirit of worship in men, or the influence which it exerts upon their concrete activities. Thus worship may be overt or direct, unconscious or conscious. Where conscious, its emotional color can range from fear through reverence to self-oblivious love. But whatever its form of expression may be, it is always a subject-object relationship; and its general existence therefore constitutes a damaging criticism of all merely subjective and immanental explanations of Reality. For worship is an acknowledgment of Transcendence, that is to say, of a Reality independent of the worshipper, which is always more or less deeply colored by mystery, and which is there first. As Von Hügel would say, it is "rooted in ontology." Or, if we prefer the witness of a modern anthropologist, even on primitive levels it at least points to man's profound sense of dependence upon "the spiritual side of the unknown."

So, directly we take this strange thing Worship seriously, and give it the status it deserves among the various responses of men to their environment, we find that it obliges us to take up a particular attitude towards that environment. Even in its crudest form, the law of prayer—indeed the fact of prayer—is already the law of belief, since humanity's universal instinct to worship cannot be accounted for, if naturalism tells the whole truth about life. That instinct means the latent recognition of a metaphysical reality, standing over against physical reality, which men are driven to adore and long to apprehend. In other words, it is the implicit, even though unrecognized Vision of God—that disclosure of the Supernatural which is overwhelming, self-giving, and attractive all at once—which is the first cause of all worship, from the puzzled upward glance of the primitive to the delighted self-oblation of the saint. Here, the human derived spirit perceives and moves towards its Origin and goal, even though that perception shares the imperfections and uncertainties of the temporal order, and is often embodied in crude and mistaken forms. Here man responds to the impact of Eternity, and in so doing learns the existence of Eternity, accepting his tiny place in that secret life of Creation, which consists in the praise, adoration, and manifestation of God. That is to say, he achieves his destiny.

These words, of course, are written from the standpoint of Christian Theism. Such a view of worship implies a developed religion; but it is a function of developed religion to speak for and interpret the inarticulate convictions of the race. It is possible to regard worship as one of the greatest of humanity's mistakes, a form taken by the fantasy-life, the desperate effort of bewildered creatures to come to terms with the surrounding mystery. Or it may be accepted as the most profound of man's responses to reality, and more than this, the organ of his divine knowledge and the earnest of eternal life. Between these two extreme positions, however, it is difficult to find a firm resting place for the mind. Nor has the religious man any choice. He is bound to take worship seriously, and ever more seriously with the deepening of his own spiritual sense. It points steadily towards the Reality of God: it gives, expresses, and maintains that which is the essence of all sane religion—a theocentric basis to life. "The first or central act of religion is *adoration*, sense of God, His otherness though nearness, His distinctness from all finite beings, though not separateness—aloofness—from them."

It is true that from first to last self-regarding elements are mixed with human worship; but these are no real part of it. Not man's needs and wishes, but God's presence and incitement, first evoke it. As it rises towards purity and leaves egotistic piety behind, He becomes more and more the only Fact of existence, the one Reality; and the very meaning of Creation is seen to be an act of worship, a devoted proclamation of the splendor, the wonder, and the beauty of God. In this great *Sanctus*, all things justify their being and have their place. God alone matters, God alone Is—creation only matters because of Him. "Wherein does your prayer consist?" said St. John of the Cross to one of his penitents. She replied: "In considering the Beauty of God, and in rejoicing that He has such beauty."

Such disinterested delight is the perfection of worship. Yet we cannot limit the word to that small group of souls capable of this effect of Charity, or even to those activities which it is usual to class as "religious." Though we find at its heart the adoring response of spirit to Spirit, its periphery is great enough to include all the expressive acts and humble submissions of men, if they are given a Godward orientation. The great outbursts of unshakable certitude and adoring love which we find upon the lips of the Saints stand up like Alpine peaks in the spiritual landscape of humanity. But the lower pastures, the deepest valleys and darkest forests, even the jungles and the swamps, are all part of the same world; they depend on the same given heat and light, the same seasonal vicissitudes. Each in its own way responds to that heat and light, and under its incitement brings forth living things. We shall not understand the mountain by treating it in isolation, nor do justice to the lower levels unless we also remember the heights. "God," says St. John of the Cross again, "passes through the thicket of the world, and wherever His glance falls He turns all things to beauty."

Worship, then, at every level, always means God and the priority of God, however thick the veils through which He is apprehended, and however grotesque the disguise He may seem to wear. Through and in a multitude of strange divinities and along lowly channels suited to the lowliness of man, the "outpouring of the Incomprehensible Grandeur," as Dionysius the Areopagite says, goes on. We in our worshipping action are compelled to move within the devotional sphere, with all its symbolic furniture, its archaic survivals, its pitfalls, its risks of sentimentalism, herd-suggestion, and disguised self-regard. But the mighty Object of our worship stands beyond and over against all this in His utter freedom and distinctness. "Can" and "cannot," "is" and "is not" must not be predicated of Him, without a virtual remembrance that these words merely refer to our limited experience and not to God as He is in Himself. If this contrast is forgotten, we shall never understand the religious scene and the strange objects with which it is bestrewn. There is no department of life which asks from those who study it so much humble sympathy, such a wide, genial, unfastidious spirit, or so constant a remembrance of our own limitations as this; nor is there one in which it is more necessary to remember the wholesome reminder of the psychologist that we ourselves, however apparently civilized, are still possessed of a primitive subconsciousness which is nowhere more active than in the practices of our religion.

If the first point about worship is its theocentric character, if its reference be always to "the Absolute and Eternal, standing beyond the present and the past," there follows from this the obvious truth that man could never have produced it in his own strength. It does not appear spontaneously from within the created order, and cannot be accounted for in terms of evolution. Strictly speaking, there is no such thing as "natural religion": the distinction which is often drawn between "natural" and "revealed" faith is an artificial one, set up by theologizing minds. That awed conviction of the reality of the Eternal over against us, that awareness of the Absolute, that sense of God, which in one form or another is the beginning of all worship, whether it seems to break in from without, or to arise within the soul, does not and cannot originate in man. It comes to him where he is, as a message from another order; God disclosing Himself to and in His creation "by diverse portions and in diverse manners" conditioned by the limitations of the humble creature He has made. It is, in fact, a Revelation, proportioned to the capacity of the creature, of something wholly other than our finite selves, and not deducible from our finite experience: the splendor and distinctness of God. Therefore the easy talk of the pious naturalist about man's approach to God, is both irrational—indeed plainly impudent—and irreverent, unless the priority of God's approach to man be kept in mind.

In this respect worship stands alone, and cannot be equated with man's other discoveries of, and reactions to, his rich and many-leveled environment. In all these, he is pressed by the needs and perils of his situation, or by the prick of his own desires, first to exploration and then to precarious adjustments with this or that aspect of a changing world. But in his worship, he is compelled as it were in spite of himself to acknowledge and respond to a Wholeness, a Perfection already fully present over against him—something, as St. Augustine says, "insusceptible of change." This contrast between the successive and the Eternal lies at the root of all worship, which ever looks away from the transitory and created to the Abiding and Eternal—not because this august Reality consoles or succors men, not because worship enriches and completes our natural life, but for Its own sake. Here even the deep religious mood of dependence and of gratitude must give priority to the fundamental religious mood of adoration. Where it is emptied of this unearthly element, this awestruck and creaturely sense of the Holy and Immortal, worship loses its most distinctive characteristic. The Seraphic hymn gives its very essence: "Holy! Holy! Holy! Lord God of hosts, heaven and earth are full of thy glory. Glory be to thee, O Lord Most High." That is worship.

It is true that this holy Reality is at first recognized by man in a very imperfect and distorted way; and acknowledged in acts which may bear little apparent resemblance to the practices which we regard as religious. Yet already these acts have the distinctive mark of worship. They point beyond the world and natural life, to an independent Object of adoration. That Transcendendent Object, even though conceived as the Cause of all natural good, and present in and with the natural scene, yet speaks to man from a realm that exceeds and stands over against all natural good; and It may incite him to deeds and renunciations which sharply oppose the interests of his natural life, and have no meaning save in so far as they point beyond the world. As man develops, its attraction and its pressure are more and more realized in contrast to those natural interests. And at last in the Saint (without whose existence worship can never be understood) the revealed Reality fills the horizon and becomes the sole object of love, so that even though God gave nothing of Himself to the soul, yet the soul must give the whole of itself to Him.

It follows from this that worship and prayer, though their relation be so close, and their overlapping so frequent, must never be treated as equivalents. For worship is essentially disinterested—it "means only God"—but prayer is only in some of its aspects disinterested. One offers, the other asks. "What shall I say, my God, my Holy Joy!" exclaims St. Augustine. There is the voice of worship. "Without thy visitation I cannot live!" says Thomas à Kempis. There is the voice of prayer. It is true that throughout the history of religion there has always been a mingling of motives; fear and anxiety, over against the all-powerful Unknown, expressed in propitiation and demand, are inevitable elements of the primitive response, and have endured to affect the whole religious history of the race. But as the genuine religious impulse becomes dominant, adoration more and more takes charge. "I come to seek God because I need Him," may be an adequate formula for prayer. "I come to adore His splendor, and fling myself and all that I have at His feet," is the only possible formula for worship. Even on the crudest levels, it has in it the seed of contemplation, and points towards self-loss.

Thus worship will include all those dispositions and deeds which adoration wakes up in us, all the responses of the soul to the Uncreated, all the Godward activities of man. Because it sets the awful Perfection of God over against the creature's imperfection, it becomes the most effective cause of "conviction of sin," and hence of the soul's penitence and purification, here disclosing its creative and transfiguring power. So, too, that strange impulse to sacrifice and unlimited self-abandonment, which is the life-blood of religion, is an expression of the worshipping instinct, and has no meaning except in relation to a supernatural goal. When we consider how unnecessary religious action is to man's physical well-being—how frequently, indeed, its demands run counter to his material advantage—yet how irresistible is its attraction for awakened souls, we can hardly doubt that here in this mysterious communion which we know from the human side as "worship," there is disclosed to us a deep purpose of the Eternal Will, and a path is opened along which our conditioned spirits can move out towards the Absolute Life.

Yet having said this, so rich and complex are those spiritual currents which penetrate and surround us, and so firm the refusal of Spirit to fit into the neat categories of thought, that we are bound to qualify the stress upon Transcendence by an acknowledgment of the many strands which enter into the worshipping life, the many paths along which God makes His approach to man, and stirs man to respond to His attraction. We are not Deists. Our worship is of a God Who acts, a Living One Who transcends what seem to us to be His laws, and has a definite relation with His creatures; One, too, who works in the depths of our being, and is self-revealed through His action in history and in nature, as well as in the soul. . . .

Liturgical worship shares with all ritual action the character of a work of art. Entering upon it, we leave the lower realism of daily life for the higher realism of a successive action which expresses and interprets eternal truth by the deliberate use of poetic and symbolic material. A liturgical service should therefore possess a structural unity, its general form and movement, and each of its parts, being determined by the significance of the whole. By its successive presentation of all the phases of the soul's response to the Holy, its alternative use of history and oratory, drama and rhythm, its appeals to feeling, thought, and will, the individual is educated and gathered into the great movement of the Church. Here intellect as well as emotion has its part to play in stirring to activity the deeper levels of the soul; for liturgy, being in its nature a corporate and stylized acknowledgement of the most august realities of our experience, must be informed by disciplined thought—again in this exhibiting its likeness to great art. Nevertheless, since its main function is to suggest the Supernatural and lead men out to communion with the Supernatural, it is by the methods of poetry that its chief work will be done. At least three-quarters of the text of the Byzantine liturgy is poetry; and though the proportion in the Roman and Anglican services is less, poetry still remains a chief element at least in the Daily Office, which is mainly an arrangement of psalms, canticles, and Scripture readings. Now poetry is not, and is not intended to be, realistic in the crude sense, though it is a chief means by which religious realism is achieved, since without its help mystery can hardly be expressed. We therefore entirely mistake its office and method if we seek to give literal meaning to its religious utterances; and this mistake, which is often made, is the basis of much criticism directed against institutional worship. . . .

There comes, for many souls, a time when those feelings, images, and considerations in which their prayer has clothed itself, and which are often regarded as the real stuff of religious experience, disclose their oblique and symbolic character, and lose in consequence their numinous quality. They can no longer be used with sincerity; and their departure, and that of the associated emotions, leaves a painful blank behind. The pressure of God now produces at best an obscure and general knowledge, at worst a painful sense of ignorance and emptiness; and the self's response, stripped of human images and conscious fervor, becomes difficult and dry. This is the "night of the senses" which is described by St. John of the Cross and other masters of the inner life. It is not a rare or lofty mystical state, but is experienced in some manner by all who make the transition from imaginative to recollected worship. God is now apprehended darkly but directly, as a Reality wholly incomprehensible by the mind, and is worshipped, as *The Cloud of Unknowing* says, by "a naked intent stretching towards Him." Yet this obscure act, apparently so empty of content— this faithful listening in the darkness—is recognized by those in whom it is produced as a genuine communion with God. For that reason, in spite of the aridity and suffering which often accompany it, it is deeply pacifying to the soul, whose worship now becomes, more and more, a simple state of loving attention to Him.

Final Retreat

1937?

NOTES IN RETREAT

No love without pain. Now am better than I have been for two years and *physically* quite capable of retreats, etc. Entirely a spiritual question as to whether I should do them. *Prioress* says: keep out of all the traffic of the world for present—very important. But this would involve not mixing with people as well as not doing jobs. When I can shut off the world—quiet days or so on—I do live at a wholly different level and gradually get into another state and attitude. But I can't keep this up in the ordinary way. So far I have nothing at all to show for reduced work and engagements except improved nervous and general health, which was *not* my object.

Mixing with theologians, etc., *does* excite and distract and give me pleasure.

On the other hand, I do know the *right path* is poverty and self-stripping. Yet I've been given, as a matter of fact and without demanding or trying for it, rather more success than usual lately. Is this just temptation or God's will?

Prayer—either utterly distracted or else silent absorption in God. These late Communions very miserable business, but will have to go on till winter ends. By the time one gets to church already distracted for the day. *Dispositions*—much too hard-hearted. I notice real people of prayer made acutely unhappy by suffering or evil, but it *never seems* to take me like that. Can't concentrate my mind on it. Though I may be rather distressed on the surface, or worried, impatient, etc., a sort of fundamental calm never disturbed, which may be and probably is, just callousness and want of love.

Ruling. All right—not my type to be afflicted. Damp everything down even if formal. Pray about the commonplace things of daily life.

1938

The retreat center at Pleshy, the English village where she declared her Christian faith, remained one of her special places. In spite of ill health, she agreed to conduct another retreat there. She meditates upon the Eucharistic liturgy as it is written in ancient service books, drawing particularly from Arthur Linton's collection of Twenty-five Consecration Prayers.

From *The Mystery of Sacrifice*

The Liturgy declares again and again that once we have entered the supernatural region it is God alone who is the mover, the doer of all that is done. He alone uplifts, renews, transforms, converts, consecrates by the independent action of His grace; and this, His consecrating action, is mostly unperceived by us. His invisible rays beat upon, penetrate, and transform the soul. Sometimes their action quietens and steadies us; sometimes it burns and convicts us, induces a profound religious discomfort which we do not understand. But the full power of those transforming rays could not be endured by us at all, if it rose to the level of consciousness and was felt by sensitive nature. The saints have sometimes spoken of it, of the awful burning of the Fire of Love, the flame of living charity that burns to heal, or the agony of the heat that purifies our desire, cleanses the thoughts of the heart, scorches and kills self-esteem. This is the real fire that burns on the altar, and into which the living sacrifice must be plunged. Outward trials, pains, renunciations, temptations, revolts are only the matter of this sacrament: appropriate to the creature, but not necessary to God. All that is needed for His purpose of consecration is the impact of the Eternal Charity in its transforming power upon the soul, that it may "receive the diadem of beauty from the Lord's hand."

When we look at the great Eucharistic prayer as we find it in its classic form in the early Liturgies—for in all our Western rites it is mangled and incomplete—we see gathered into this one supreme act of worship all the strands that make up the Godward life of man. "A sacrifice," said St. Augustine, "is an act or rite performed in order that we may inhere in God", and here is the central point at which oblation merges into sacrifice, to be completed by the communion of the human and the divine. In form the prayer is a great doxology addressed to the Triune Majesty of the Godhead, Transcendent, Incarnate, Immanent: a delighted and awestruck proclamation of the infinite Perfection of God, and of reliance on the merciful action of God. It has three closely interdependent parts. First it moves out towards Eternity, and joins the "unsilenced praise" of the spiritual universe, offering with angels and archangels, the unseen powers and presences of the supernatural order, adoration and thanksgiving to God for His Being, His holiness, His self-revelation to men. So the Nestorian priest at the opening of the Canon:

"With those heavenly hosts we also, gracious Lord, O God the merciful Father, even we cry out and say: Holy art thou indeed and holy art thou in truth, and lofty art thou and exalted above all, who hast made thy worshippers on earth worthy to become like those who glorify thee in heaven!"

Then, gathering herself to that which is for her the focal point of this mighty scene of cosmic worship, as in the vision of the Apocalypse all centers on the altar of the lamb, the Church remembers and gives thanks for the cause of her very being: God's saving action within the world of time, the "eternal birth from the Godhead of the Only Begotten," and the historic Incarnation and Passion of Christ. For the appeal to history is of the very stuff of Christian worship, which cannot express itself in abstract terms alone. Therefore we here present before God the memorial of the greatest moment of our history: when in and for the human race Christ made the perfect response of love, and carried humanity in His Person up into Eternal Life. Here the Liturgy displays to the soul the austere attractions of a total self-abandonment, the Cross, and the reward of the Cross. "Offering unto Thee this saving Mystery of the Body and Blood of Thine Only-Begotten Son, we recall the sufferings that He endured for our salvation."

And now the Church, concelebrating with her Master, and again and again setting forth within the visible order the unseen mystery of His eternal sacrifice, adds solemn commemorative action to solemn commemorative words. As He "the day before He suffered took bread into His holy and venerable hands," and giving thanks blessed and brake it, so she "having in mind the blessed Passion," blesses in like manner the oblation of bread and wine, and offers it to God, praying that these gifts, now consecrated and become "the Bread of Eternal Life and the Chalice of everlasting Salvation," may be presented in their reality at "Thine Altar on high, in the presence of Thy Divine Majesty." And last, the triune action is completed by the invocation of the Holy Spirit, that He may come in the splendor of His life-giving power, and "rest upon, bless, and hallow" the Offering and the offerers, and unify in God Eternity and Time.

In this great prayer—which is indeed the prayer of the whole Church, for here the priest acts as the representative of the people, and in the Dialogue, the Sanctus, and the great Amen the people take their part—we reach the very heart of Christian worship. For Christian worship is, essentially, a consecration. In it man with his whole being, of soul and of body, and as the head of all creation, adores God and gives himself to God. And he is enabled to do this because in his name and for His necessity, the incarnate Logos, standing beside His creature and accepting its limitations, has consecrated Himself. "Thou didst put on our humanity that Thou mightest quicken us by Thy Divinity," says the ancient liturgy of Saints Adai and Mari. Thus the dramatic commemoration of the life and death of the Incarnate must stand at the very center of the rite, with its reminder of the sacred efficacy of suffering, its deep humanity, and its rebuke to mere other-worldliness. One Figure in whom the deepest meanings of sacrifice are fulfilled, set at one point in space and time, is the cause of our adoration and the Offerer of the Church's sacrifice. "As the bread once scattered on the tops of the mountains when gathered together came to be one," says the Eucharistic prayer of Serapion, so the souls of men are gathered on this altar and held up to God in a single sacrifice of love.

This august sequence, which is yet one single act of consecration, has its close parallel in the secret experience of the soul; for all the aspects under which the Godhead has revealed Itself must have a part in the creature's sanctification. Here too we are first led out to the adoration which shall express the total Godward temper of our life, the awed and delighted contemplation of Reality, which includes, penetrates, and transforms all action. Then within this worship, we are called to the perpetual remembrance and the faithful study of a pattern of sacrificial love, placed within our own order and subject to our own conditions: the bit by bit imitation of Christ and slow incorporation into the mystery of Christ. For the work of sanctification as experienced by us in time is successive, as the consecrating action in the Eucharistic is successive. God the Sanctifier is simultaneous and eternal; but man the sanctified is ever subject to the law of growth and change. Nor does this growth and this change lie within his own capacity. Having offered himself to the Transforming Love, he has done what he is able to do. It is the Spirit, the Lord and Giver of life, coming to rest upon the offering, which sanctifies and changes by His deep mysterious action that humanity which of itself is nothing, and yet is capable of all.

A consecrated life is not, then, something to which the soul can attain even by the most steadfast and devoted action of the dedicated will. It is something which we cannot achieve by our own efforts, and yet for which we were made. The secret Eucharistic action brings us, through self-offering to God and self-spending for men, to adoring joy, to a humble and grateful memorial of the saving action of God— and thence by the operation of the Spirit to an entire transformation in Him. It does not follow that this transforming action is perceptible to that which is transformed. The formula of real abandonment is not "Leave all, so that something may happen, some spiritual reward be gained." There is a full stop after "all": the issue is left wholly in the hands of God. Often it seems to the soul as if nothing happens. It is weak, finite, ineffective as before. So the victim on the Cross showed no marks of victory; nor does the bread upon the altar know that it has become the matter of a sacrament, when it is taken up, broken, and made an instrument of self-imparting life.

Thus the soul giving itself to the Eucharistic action is seldom aware of all the implications of its destiny. Neither can it always recognize under earthly disguises the consecrating touch of the "holy and venerable hands." It has given itself to become part of that total sacrifice, the worship which creation offers to its Origin: a worship summed up in Christ, presented at His altar, and perpetuated in His Church. What its particular part in that solemn oblation may be, is not for it to choose or ask to know. Eager for action, it may be forced to passivity; or, craving for deeper communion with God, it may be sent out to serve and teach the world. It may be called to the awful fear and reluctance of Gethsemane, when the full demands of God are disclosed. It may be asked to bear the cowardice or disloyalty of those who seemed faithful, the sharp blow of physical pain, the humiliating disability to carry the Cross, or to accept apparent failure as the very condition of Divine victory—the darkness and forsakenness of Calvary, its human weakness and despair. Insistent demands on its rescuing love may have to be met when they are least able to be borne. These various and disconcerting disciplines, frustrations, sufferings, confusions of mind and failures of body, fear, weariness, loss of prayer, do not alienate the surrendered soul from God. They bring it nearer to Him by the only safe path. They are or can be the occasions of its consecration, its share in the sacrificial life through and in which redeeming love is poured out upon the world.

Correspondence

LETTER TO VIOLET HOLDSWORTH

Though I am not yet half-way through the sixties, illness plus age has come to mean a very thorough limitation of freedom, and general slowing down, and dependence upon others; none of which is altogether easy to a person who prefers to do everything for herself at express speed. But it's a marvelous discipline, and introduces one to a completely fresh series of tests and opportunities, and involves the discovery of so much devoted kindness.

LETTERS TO E. I. WATKIN

Don't you find these times very difficult for pacifists? The War seems to enter into everything, and there are few things that one can conscientiously do. Most of my quasi pacifist friends are becoming more warlike, apparently feeling that provocation is more important than principles, and that the only way to combat sin in others is to commit sin ourselves. The attitude of the Anglican Bishops has been disappointing, though a great many of the clergy are strongly pacifist.

❧

I am supposed to be writing a book on Christianity and the Spiritual Life for the Christian Challenge series, but feel quite unable to get on with it partly because a long stretch of ill health has reduced my vitality, partly the difficulty of living in somebody else's house, as we are doing now with only a few of my books.

Abba

Though published late in her life, Abba is based on retreat addresses delivered in 1935. She reworked these ideas and presented us with her final comments on prayer.

From *Abba*

It is too often supposed that when our Lord said, "In this manner pray ye," He meant not "these are the right dispositions and longings, the fundamental acts of every soul that prays," but "this is the form of words which, above all others, Christians are required to repeat." As a consequence this is the prayer in which, with an almost incredible stupidity, they have found the material of those vain repetitions which He has specially condemned. Again and again in public and private devotion the Lord's Prayer is taken on hurried lips, and recited at a pace which makes impossible any realization of its tremendous claims and profound demands. Far better than this cheapening of the awful power of prayer was the practice of the old woman described by St. Teresa, who spent an hour over the first two words, absorbed in reverence and love.

It is true, of course, that this pattern in its verbal form, its obvious and surface meaning, is far too familiar to us. Rapid and frequent repetition has reduced it to a formula. We are no longer conscious of its mysterious beauty and easily assume that we have long ago exhausted its inexhaustible significance. The result of this persistent error has been to limit our understanding of the great linked truths which are here given to us; to harden their edges, and turn an instruction which sets up a standard for each of the seven elements of prayer, and was intended to govern our whole life towards God, into a set form of universal obligation.

This is a sovereign instance of that spiritual stupidity with which we treat the "awful and mysterious truths" religion reveals to us, truths of which Coleridge has rightly said, that they are commonly "considered so true as to lose all the powers of truth, and lie bedridden in the dormitory of the soul." But when we "center down," as Quakers say, from the surface of human life to its deeps, and rouse those sleeping truths and take them with us, and ask what they look like there—in the secret place where the soul is alone with God and knows its need of God—then, all looks different. These great declarations disclose their intensity of life, their absolute quality, as a work of art which has hung respected and unloved in a public gallery glows with new meaning when we bring it into the home or the sanctuary for which it was really made. Seen thus, the Lord's Prayer reminds us how rich and various, how deeply rooted in the Supernatural, the Christian life is or should be, moving from awestruck worship to homely confidence, and yet one: how utterly it depends on God, yet how searching is the demand it makes on man. "Every just man," says Osuna, "needs the seven things for which this prayer—or this scheme of prayer—asks." Taken together they cover all the realities of our situation, at once beset by nature and cherished by grace, establishing Christian prayer as a relation between wholes, between man in his completeness and God who is all.

And we note their order and proportion. First, four clauses entirely concerned with our relation to God; then three concerned with our human situation and needs. Four hinge on the First Commandment, three hinge on the Second. Man's twisted, thwarted and embittered nature, his state of sin, his

sufferings, helplessness, and need, do not stand in the foreground, but the splendor and beauty of God, demanding a
self-oblivion so complete that it transforms suffering, and
blots out even the memory of sin. We begin with a sublime
yet intimate invocation of Reality, which plunges us at once
into the very ground of the Universe and claims kinship with
the enfolding mystery. Abba, Father. The Infinite God is the
Father of my soul. We end by the abject confession of our
dependence and need of guidance: of a rescue and support
coming to our help right down in the jungle of life. Following
the path of the Word Incarnate, this prayer begins on the
summits of spiritual experience and comes steadily down
from the Infinite to the finite, from the Spaceless to the little
space on which we stand. Here we find all the strange mixed
experience of man, over-ruled by the unchanging glory and
charity of God.

The crowds who followed Christ hoping for healing or
counsel did not ask Him to teach them how to pray; nor did
He give this prayer to them. It is not for those who want
religion to be helpful, who seek after signs, those who expect
it to solve their political problems and cure their diseases, but
are not prepared to share its cost. He gave it to those whom
He was going to incorporate into His rescuing system, use in
His ministry: the sons of the Kingdom, self-given to the
creative purposes of God. "*Thou* when thou prayest . . . pray
ye on this manner." It is the prayer of those "sent forth" to
declare the Kingdom, whom the world will hate, whose
unpopularity with man will be in proportion to their loyalty
to God, the apostles of the Perfect in whom, if they are true
to their vocation, the Spirit of the Father will speak. The
disciples sent out to do Christ's work were to depend on
prayer, an unbroken communion with the Eternal; and this
is the sort of prayer on which they were to depend. We
therefore, when we dare to use it, offer ourselves by

implication as their fellow workers for the Kingdom, for it supposes and requires an unconditional and filial devotion to the interests of God. Those who use the prayer must pray from the Cross.

Men have three wants, which only God can satisfy. They need food, for they are weak and dependent. They need forgiveness, for they are sinful. They need guidance, for they are puzzled. Give—Forgive—Lead—Deliver. All their prayer can be reduced to the loving adoration of the Father and the confident demand for His help.

If the transforming power of religion is to be felt, its discipline must be accepted, its price paid in every department of life; and it is only when the soul is awakened to the reality and call of God, known at every point of its multiple experience, that it is willing to pay the price and accept the discipline. Worship is a primary means of this awakening.

It follows once more that whole-hearted adoration is the only real preparation for right action: action which develops within the Divine atmosphere, and is in harmony with the eternal purposes of God. The Bible is full of illustrations of this truth, from the call of Isaiah to the Annunciation. First the awestruck recognition of God, and then, the doing of His Will. We cannot discern His Eternal Purpose, even as it affects our tiny lives, opportunities and choices, except with the eyes of disinterested and worshipping love. The hallowing of the Name is therefore the essential condition without which it is not possible to work for the Kingdom or recognize the pressure of the Will. So the first imperative of the life of prayer is that which the humanist finds so hard to understand. We are to turn our backs upon earth, and learn how to deal with its sins and its needs by looking steadfastly up to heaven.

Yet the life of prayer is incomplete if it stops here, in the realm of aspiration. Costly action as well as delighted fervor must form part of it. Like all else in the spiritual life of animal man, it must have its sacramental expression. Heroic sacrifice, peaceful suffering, patient and inconspicuous devotion to uncongenial tasks, the steady fight against sin, ugliness, squalor, and disease, the cleansing of national thought and increase of brotherhood among men: all this is our response to the impact of Perfection, our active recognition of the claim of God. Awe alone is sterile. But when it is married to sacrificial love, the fruits of the Spirit begin to appear; and the hallowing of the Name and the working for the Kingdom are seen to be two sides of one reality—the response of the creature to the demand of Love.

Having recognized and worshipped the Name, we pray next for its triumph: Thy Kingdom come. Here man's most sacred birthright, his deep longing for perfection, and with it his bitter consciousness of imperfection, break out with power. We want to bring the God whom we worship, His beauty, His sovereignty, His order, into the very texture of our life, and the fundamental human need for action into the radius of our prayer. This is the natural sequel to the prayer of adoration. We have had a glimpse of the mystery of the Holy, have worshipped before the veils of beauty and sacrifice; and that throws into vivid relief the poverty, the anarchy, the unreality in which we live—the resistance of the world, the creature to God, and its awful need of God.

Thy Kingdom come! We open our gates to the Perfect, and entreat its transfiguring presence, redeeming our poor contingencies, our disharmonies, making good our perpetual fallings short. We face the awful contrast between the Actual and the Real, and acknowledge our need of deliverance from sin, especially that sin of the world, that rebellion of creation against the Holy, which has thrust us out of heaven. The

Kingdom is the serenity of God already enfolding us, and seeking to penetrate and redeem the whole of this created order, "shattering the horror of perpetual night" by a ray of heavenly brightness. We pray for this transformation of life, this healing of its misery and violence, its confusion and unrest, through the coming of the Holy God whom we adore, carrying through to regions still unconquered the great, the primary petition for the hallowing of His Name. That the Splendor over against us may enter, cleanse, and sanctify every level of our existence, give it a new quality, coherence, and meaning.

The prayer is not that we may come into the Kingdom, for this we cannot do in our own strength. It is that the Kingdom, the Wholly Other, may come to us, and become operative within our order: one thing working in another, as leaven in our dough, as seed in our field. We are not encouraged to hope that the social order will go on evolving from within, until at last altruism triumphs and greed is dethroned: nor indeed does history support this view. So far is this amiable program from the desperate realities of our situation, so unlikely is it that human nature will ever do the work of grace, that now we entreat the Divine Power to enter history by His Spirit and by His saints, to redeem, cleanse, fertilize, and rule.

What we look for then is not Utopia, but something which is given from beyond: Emmanuel, God with us, the whole creation won from rebellion and consecrated to the creative purposes of Christ. This means something far more drastic than the triumph of international justice and good social conditions. It means the transfiguration of the natural order by the supernatural: by the Eternal Charity. Though we achieve social justice, liberty, peace itself, though we give our bodies to be burned for these admirable causes, if we lack this we are nothing. For the Kingdom is the Holy, not the moral;

the Beautiful, not the correct; the Perfect, not the adequate; Charity, not law.

Thus more and more we must expect our small action to be overruled and swallowed up in the vast Divine action, and be ready to offer it, whatever it may be, for the fulfillment of God's purpose, however much this may differ from our purpose. The Christian turns again and again from that bewildered contemplation of history in which God is so easily lost, to the prayer of filial trust in which He is always found, knowing here that those very things which seem to turn to man's disadvantage, may yet work to the Divine advantage. On the frontier between prayer and history stands the Cross, a perpetual reminder of the price by which the Kingdom is brought in. Seen from the world's side it is foolishness; seen from the land of contemplation, it is the Wisdom of God. We live in illusion till that wisdom has touched us; and this touch is the first coming of the Kingdom to the individual soul.

None can guess beforehand with what anguish, what tearing of old hard tissues and habits, the Kingdom will force a path into the soul, and confront self-love in its last fortress with the penetrating demand of God. Yet we cannot use the words, unless we are prepared to pay this price: nor is the prayer of adoration real, unless it leads on to this. When we said, "Hallowed be Thy Name!" we acknowledged the priority of Holiness. Now we offer ourselves for the purposes of Holiness, handing ourselves over to God that His purposes, great or small, declared or secret, natural or spiritual, may be fulfilled through us and in us, and all that is hostile to His Kingdom done away.

To look with real desire for the coming of the Kingdom means crossing over to God's side, dedicating our powers, whatever they may be, to the triumph of His purpose. The Bible is full of a stern insistence on that action which is ever the corollary of true contemplation. It is here that the praying spirit accepts its most sacred privilege: active and costly cooperation with God—first in respect of its own purification, and then in respect of His creative and redeeming action upon life. Our attitude here must be wide open towards God, exhibiting quite simply our poverty and impurity, acknowledging our second-rateness, but still offering ourselves such as we are. Thy Kingdom come! Here am I, send me. Not the nature-lover's admiration but the laborer's hard work turns the corn-field into the harvest-field. Hard work, which soon loses the aura of romantic devotion, and must be continued through drudgery and exhaustion to the end.

Last Letters

LETTER TO L. K.

I am still in my room but am up at last allowed to do nix
and hardly move as everything makes me breathless, it
transpires that the long illness destroyed the elasticity of
my lungs and that takes ages to come back (so far as it does
come back), meanwhile one just has to stay put, and submit
to having everything done for one. I can't say I like it
much but it seems to be the Lord's idea for the present
moment.

FROM HER LAST LETTERS IN A TIME OF WAR

Just plain self-forgetfulness is the greatest of graces. The true
relation between the soul and God is the perfectly simple one
of childlike dependence. Well then, *be* simple and dependent,
acknowledge once and for all the plain fact that you have
nothing of our own, offer your life to God and trust Him with
the ins and outs of your soul as well as everything else!
Cultivate a loving relation to Him in your daily life; don't
be ferocious with yourself, because that is treating badly a
precious if imperfect thing which God has made.

At present, I think one can do little but try to live in charity, and do what one can for the suffering and bewildered. We are caught up in events far too great for us to grasp, and which have their origin in the demonic powers of the spiritual world. Let us hope that the end of all the horror and destruction may be a purification of life.

༈

I remain pacifist but I quite see that at present the Christian world is not there. Like you I feel the final synthesis must reconcile the lion and the lamb—but meanwhile the crescendo of horror and evil and wholesale destruction of beauty is hard to accept.

༈

Anyhow I do feel that trusting God *must* mean trusting Him through thick and thin.

Essay

The Mystic and the Corporate Life

One of the commonest of the criticisms which are brought against the mystics is that they represent an unsocial type of religion; that their spiritual enthusiasms are personal and individual, and that they do not share or value the corporate life and institutions of the Church or community to which they belong. Yet, as a matter of fact, the relation that does and should exist between personal religion and the corporate life of the Church frequently appears in them in a peculiarly intense, a peculiarly interesting form; and in their lives, perhaps, more easily than elsewhere, we may discern the principles which do or should govern the relation of the individual to the community.

In true mystics, who are so often and so wrongly called "religious individualists," we see personal religion raised to its highest power. If we accept their experience as genuine, it involves an intercourse with the spiritual world, an awareness of it, which transcends the normal experience, and appears to be independent of the general religious consciousness of the community to which they belong. Mystics speak with God as persons with a Person, and not as members of a group. They live by an immediate knowledge far more than by belief, by a knowledge achieved in those hours of direct, unmediated intercourse with the Transcendent when, as they say, they were "in union with God." The certitude then gained— a certitude which they cannot impart, and which is not generally diffused—governs all their reactions to the universe. It even persists and upholds them in those terrible hours of darkness when all their sense of spiritual reality is taken away.

Such a personality as this seems at first sight to stand in little need of the support which the smaller nature, the more languid religious consciousness, receives from the corporate spirit. By the very term "mystic" we indicate a certain aloofness from the crowd, suggest that they are in possession of a secret which the community as a whole does not and cannot share, that they live at levels to which others cannot rise. I think that much of the distrust with which they are often regarded comes from this sense of their independence of the herd, their apparent separation from the often clumsy and always symbolic methods of institutional religion, and the further fact that their own methods and results cannot be criticized or checked by those who have not shared them. "I spake as I saw," said David; and those who did not see can only preserve a respectful or an exasperated silence.

Yet this common opinion that mystics are lonely souls wholly absorbed in their vertical relation with God, that their form of religious life represents an opposition to, and an implicit criticism of, the corporate and institutional form of religious life—this is decisively contradicted by history, which shows us, again and again, the great mystics as the loyal children of the great religious institutions, and forces us to admit that here as in other departments of human activity the corporate and the individual life are intimately plaited together. . . .

Excerpts from *The Gray World*

Most children of the normal type have their moments of mysticism, when their spirit first stirs and they wonder what they really are, puzzling over memory and consciousness and other things which elude their rudimentary language, but which they take it for granted that their elders know all about. Master Hopkinson, always acutely conscious of two worlds equally near to him, pondered perhaps less on these things, because to him they were so obvious, objectionable, and distinct. In later and more articulate years he was accustomed to say that he came to his infancy trailing clouds which had no elements of glory. The phrase was accurate, and he did not find its literary associations disagreeable.

The Gray World was the warp on which the bright threads of his sensuous existence were spread—a strange and tiresome plan, perhaps; but to him profoundly natural, because it was the only one that he had ever known. But this sudden discovery that the rest of the family did not share his knowledge, live the same dual life, or frequent the same dim country, startled and distressed him. He had taken it for granted that he was as all other little boys; now it seemed clear that he had made a huge mistake. Instead of sharing with the others an experience as ordinary and inevitable as a cold in the head or a dose of powder, he was quite alone in his visits to the crowded country, and even in his memories of the time when he was one of its inhabitants. He had seen quite plainly that the Hopkinson family and its friends knew nothing of these things. Even his mother, that monument of infallibility, had seemed deeply astonished by what he himself regarded as his extremely ordinary remarks.

It was very bewildering, for he could really see no reason why he should be different from everybody else. He felt something of the helpless disgust of the seasoned traveler who comes home to find his truthful narrative received with sardonic smiles; or of the long-suffering chemist who tries to demonstrate radium before the hostile grins of a canny but uneducated audience.

At the same time, the human element in him was rather ashamed, and frightened by its temerity, and struggled to assure him that grown-up people must know everything; and the conviction grew that it was best to endure the slur on his veracity in silence, and only be careful in his own interests to steer clear of these complications in the future. After all, if for some inconceivable reason the rest of his acquaintances inhabited one world only, did not know where they had come from, and never dreamed of troubling about it, it was not to be expected that on the testimony of one small boy they should believe in truths which were to them both imperceptible and offensive.

And the Gray World was so monstrous, so impossible unless one had been there, that often when he was boat-sailing in Kensington Gardens, or when the jam roly poly pudding at dinner was particularly solid and good, Willie found it very hard to believe in it himself. That all the bright colors he loved: the nice flat blue poppies with yellowy-brown leaves which sprawled over the drawing-room paper, the scarlet of the local omnibus, and all the loveliness of sunshine and gas-light: should be shams which hid the horrible place of unending nothingness that lay in and through the streets and houses, and filled the air he breathed with melancholy ghosts—this would have been quite ridiculous if it had not happened to be true. So he excused Mrs.

Hopkinson and her callers for their ignorance; and, half in a fit of outraged dignity, and half because he dreaded the naturalistic standpoint of Pauline, he decided to avoid all references to his own thoughts and experiences until he was quite sure that the rest of the world was likely to believe in them.

As the double life that he led rather detached Master Hopkinson from a vivid interest in ordinary boy-pleasures, and made him visionary and given to quiet delights, and as Mr. and Mrs. Hopkinson strenuously upheld the policy of only talking to the children about things that children should and could understand, this resulted in his becoming an unpleasantly silent little boy. For the grip of the Unseen on his soul enlarged as he grew older, and with it his terror of betraying himself.

So he lived for the next year or two a cautious, artificial life, and all remembrance of the At Home day episode gradually faded from the family mind. They said that he was a queer child, and hoped he was going to be clever; and as Pauline outgrew the nursery, he was left a good deal to himself.

He was certainly odd in his ways, given to long hours of brooding and sudden flashes of conviction. Dream was seldom absent from his eyes, but fortunately Mrs. Hopkinson did not recognize it under that name. He loved to read the old romances and tales of King Arthur's knights, for a peculiar inarticulate joy that they gave him: but when he tried to find out the source of his fascination, he could not. Specially the story of the Holy Grail attracted him. Though his reason told him that it and the others were as untrue, as shadowy, as the rest of life, his soul found in them some secret element which nourished it and gave it peace.

He got the habit of looking into every book that he could find, for he had somehow acquired the idea that books were real, though people, he knew, were not. One day, he found a thin volume of verse, left probably by some chance visitor—Mr. Hopkinson discouraged, without difficulty, the reading of poetry by his household; he thought it dangerous stuff. This book Willie opened, and read, among much unintelligible loveliness, the following quatrain:

"We are no other than a moving row
Of Magic Shadow-shapes that come and go
 Round with the Sun-illumined Lantern held
 In Midnight by the Master of the Show."

"Then there is some one else who knows!" he thought; and went away companioned and less lonely for that knowledge. He had a constant longing to fathom the depths of the gulf which divided him from other people, though he dared not venture further confidences to discover if he really stood alone.

Sometimes he wondered if there were not other children in the same unhappy position; but he dreaded being laughed at, and the small boys at his day-school did not strike him as promising subjects for inquiry.

The solid trust in appearances which the "grown-ups" showed, and specially his father's attitude toward life, bothered him more and more. To live in the midst of superior and authoritative persons who persistently grasp the shadow and assert that it is the substance, is aggravating to an apostle, but appalling to a nervous child. Mr. Hopkinson was thought by his neighbors to be an alarmingly clever man: modern science was his god, and Huxley the high-priest of his temple, but he had a way with heretics which savored more of theology than of reason.

≒

"These obstinate questionings
Of sense and outward things,
Fallings from us, vanishings;

Blank misgivings of a creature
Moving about in worlds not realized."
WORDSWORTH

The influence of Mrs. Levi on her disciple was soon
perceptible. She raised his standard of taste, without
conferring a corresponding benefit on his morals. The result
was of doubtful advantage to a person who still lacked the
power of omitting ugly externals from his visionary field. In
effect, Mr. Willie Hopkinson became more dreamy and even
less agreeable to his neighbors than of old.

His mind had passed from the condition of boredom to
that of unrest. It hungered for Elsa's society, and for the
stimulus of her disturbing ideals, excluding her from the
verdict of hollowness which it passed on the rest of creation.
She was the one fixed point of his universe, and, wandering
from that, he felt lost. He cherished her occasional letters,
and valued the touch of her hand, with an inconsistent
materialism which he realized but was not able to kill. He
forsook the old dull poise of disillusion, but found no new
one. He began to grow, too, with a spiritual growth, painful
and spasmodic, for his soul, though always conscious, had
developed little since the childish times when it first woke to
its own existence. Its powers, beyond those of mere panic,
were immature. It perceived, but could not coordinate. It was
still the baby spirit, the troublesome, precocious child, which
takes notice easily, but holds nothing in a comprehensive
grasp. Its little fits of fear, its glimpses of the veil, and
shuddering acknowledgments of the Gray Country where
the dead search the fields of life for something to love, were
cast in petty lines. Lacking as yet the Great Companion,
Willie walked only with the dim reflection of his own mean
little soul.

It was under the direction of his Egeria that he now
began to brood upon artistic problems, to read the "Studio"

and the "Artist," and to pay secret visits to the National
Gallery. From these he returned ill-tempered and disconsolate,
tired out by uninstructed efforts to appreciate medieval art.
He found little which accorded with his preconceived idea of
the beautiful. Mrs. Levi, perhaps overestimating his intelligence, had directed his attention to Memlinck and to
Gherard David, to Duccio and to Botticelli; and he spent
puzzled hours before masterpieces as far beyond his
apprehension as he was beyond that of his relations. Only
the quiet of the place pleased him and compelled his respect;
speaking as silence will of the idea which lies beyond appearance.
He had been in other years with his mother and Pauline to
the Academy; and he remembered the discord with which
the pictures seemed to shout from the walls. Here there was
the peace of mutual courtesy. So, coming for art, he stayed
for serenity; and still influences began their slow civilizing
work upon his soul.

Stephen Miller, in another direction, gave a helping
hand to the extrication of his spirit from the marshlands of
vegetative life. Their friendship grew, slowly and carefully.
Both youths suffered from family criticism; they had been led
to think their most ordinary actions eccentric; and this gave
a coyness to their early advances. Even immortal spirits
dislike being laughed at. The emotion conceived on the dim
stairway of the Searchers of the Soul could not at first endure
a cold and unbecoming daylight.

Not, indeed, till he had been introduced into Stephen's
family circle did Willie discover how valuable were the
peculiar qualities of his friend. They seemed to have been
prepared for one another by a good-natured and discriminating
Providence. Stephen had been reared, like himself, in an
atmosphere of overpowering solidity. But his home was
opulent. There were wide passages, and two footmen.
Circumstances were easier for him than they had been for

Mr. Willie Hopkinson, though scarcely more inspiring. His father was a thin, radiant old gentleman, who seldom gave himself the trouble of rebuking his son; who read "Punch" through carefully every Tuesday night, and the "Referee" on Sundays, smiling silently at every joke. He refused to give any serious attention to the eccentricities of the young.

"Stephen," he said to Willie in the course of his first visit, "has run through all the religions, and now he's reduced to the freaks."

This, as Willie later discovered, was an exaggeration. Mr. Stephen Miller had retained the fragrance, if not the dogma, of the cults by which he had passed; and morsels culled from the "Upanishads," the "Book of the Dead," and the "Acta Sanctorum" embellished his view of the world. Each new religion, he said, gave him the sight of a fresh angle in the polygon of truth: a figure of which old Mr. Miller, safely established in the shrewd materialism of middle age, probably doubted the existence.

Stephen and Willie, however, were little bound by the limitations of their elders. Each obtained early, if vague, assurance of the other's interest in spiritual things, and bridges were soon established between them. Superior young persons often pride themselves on isolation while they pine for comradeship. The flattering comprehension of an elder woman still leaves gaps to be filled. Willie had room for Stephen; and Stephen, whose spiritual life was dominated by a lively and eclectic curiosity, eagerly desired the exploration of his friend's soul.

But Mr. Willie Hopkinson preserved a certain reticence. Stephen, he saw, followed every occult clue, however bizarre the colors of the thread, and seldom refused his hand to an unproved proposition. He did not wish his own story to take rank with these experiments. Stephen's spirit, greedy for truth and sensible of its nearness, looked toward him hopefully;

but though it seemed sad that so intelligent a person should share the delusions of the rest of the world, he avoided its contact.

Stephen argued his way toward the light by intellectual effort; did not perceive as Willie did, naturally and irrationally, the Gray World folded in the shadow-world of sense. One could not conceive of his giving to spiritual presences the same cool assent that he accorded to the tables and chairs. Yet as realities they were equally substantial. His universe was still a concrete affair; his diligent dreams no more than the expression of an esthetic unsatisfied mind. He wished to know the beyond as children wish to see fairies, because he believed it to be strange, beautiful, exciting.

They went together fairly regularly to the meetings of the Searchers of the Soul. Each had a secret hope that the absurdities of that society might one day draw from the other an indignant protest, and incidentally confession of faith. It seemed a flint on which, at any moment, one might strike out the spark of truth. And it was, finally, in some such way that they did actually come to understanding of each other.

It was an evening in which the tone of the meeting had been one of great intellectual as well as atmospheric stuffiness. The dogmatism of the dark ages, wedded to the unbridled speculation of the present, had exalted the imagination and paralyzed the intelligence of the society—"The heirs of all the ages in the foremost ranks of time," as Mr. Vincent Dawes had happily observed in his eloquent speech. Table-turning, astrology, and divination by coffee-grounds had all been called in to provide a facile solution to the great conundrum. Willie and Stephen, escaping at last from the fumes of gas and the sounds of aerated oratory, stepped from that squalid stairway, with its suggestion of putty and cheap lodgings, straight into the austere pageant of the night.

They stood upon the threshold, amazed and comforted by the purity which the west wind blows from a dark sky. It was such an abrupt change as Dante felt when he came out from hell *"a riveder le stelle"* [upon seeing the stars again]. The moon rode high above London. Little clouds, hurrying across the heavens, became opalescent poems as they approached her—faded to gray prose as they rushed away. Bathed in that milky radiance, the town, coiled in massy folds of black and of ashy gray, hid its shameful outlines as well as it might. In the great west road electric lamps blazed with an angry blue fire, trying to put out the splendors of the sky: but the moon looked down on them serenely and was not afraid. Under that heaven, so secret and so white, one seemed to imagine wide spaces of quiet and happy country at rest; and the black shadow of London—man's ugly attempt to build himself a world—lying like a blot in the midst, yet sharing in the same merciful dispensation of darkness and light. The spirit of London was awed, too, by the guardianship of this cold and gracious moon, as never by the brightness of the sun. Even the traffic went with a muffled tread. Cities dream on a moonlit night: and in their dream they smile and become beautiful.

"On a night like this," said Stephen, "so magical and still, one is almost tempted to wonder if anything is real. These streets aren't the same streets now—their essence isn't the same—as in daytime. And who's to say which is the real street?"

"It's we who are different," said Willie. "And so we see another world."

"I wonder? Do you think the other Searchers of the Soul will see what we see now?"

Willie laughed.

"Quaint persons, those," he observed.

"Quaint? Horrible! They make me ill! Always making a

pretense of wanting to know, talking of the powers of the spirit and all that—words they don't even know the fringe of. Want to know! I want to know—you want to know. We're in earnest. But they only want to gabble."

"They used to disgust me at first," answered Willie, "because I had expected them to be genuine. Don't you understand? One's always hoping for companionship. It seems incredible that every one should be blind. But now they rather amuse me. Most burlesque is built on the ashes of tragedy. I like to sit and listen, and wonder what would happen if one got up and told them the truth."

"They would say that they couldn't accept it without investigation, and that the vice-president's hypothesis was more in accordance with their spiritual intuitions."

"Probably it is."

"Oh," said Stephen, suddenly and violently. "Look! Look at the wonder and the mystery of it all! The great stars and the darkness; and the strange, careless, cruel earth. It must be different really; more ordered, more sane. Will one ever find the thing itself?"

"Better not. You're happiest in the searching."

⇥

It is a disability of the hurried children of Time that—make as they may an illusion of the hours—the boundary of each moment is for them firmly set. The angels, whose day is timeless, do not feel this. Theirs is the delicious leisure of eternity, and that is why they sometimes judge our omissions rather harshly. They cannot understand that time given to the outer is taken from the inner life; that to earn one's living it is often necessary to pauperize one's soul. They would laugh were they told that in modern life no hour has been left for reverie: that it has been given, perhaps, to physical culture, or chip-carving, or local politics. Rational religion, the Broad

Church, and other expressions of our spiritual state, do not claim rights for meditation. It is hustled out of sight to make room for more useful hobbies, and the eye of the soul becomes dim in consequence.

⚞

He felt himself to be, not any more the man in the world, but the pilgrim soul, footing it between the stars. He was walking alone, sturdily self-dependent, through exquisite landscape toward an appointed goal. That, surely, should be his life. That *was* life—a journey upon the great highway of the world toward an abiding city. A journey to be taken joyfully and in gratitude because of the beauty of the road. He conceived now of the world, of the body, as momentary conditions in the infinite progress of the spirit. Used rightly, a discipline, an initiation; used wrongly, a peril whose deeps he had once known. His idealism had come to this; to a guarded, tolerant acquiescence in the queer distorting medium of his senses, a willingness within limits to accept their reports. But it was the holy, the beautiful aspect of things that he asked them to show him. That was significant, true. No illusion of time and space, but an eternal thing which it was the very business of matter to shadow forth, the duty of that pilgrim soul in him to apprehend. One must not arrive at the Continuing City deaf and blind to the music and the radiance, obsessed by the incident worries of life. That was to have passed through the Great University in vain.

Willie was beginning to recover from the disease of spiritual self-seeking, which had crippled his first years. He had seen, at last, the face of the Great Companion. He knew what he wanted; the constant presence of that mysterious guide, the constant assurance of a strange but enduring amity. He had come to the second, or illuminative, stage of the journey; for his way, after all, had been the old mystic's way. There is no other practicable path for those who are determined on reality, who have found out the gigantic deception we accept as the visible world, the gigantic foolishness of our comfortable common-sense. The old formula came back to his mind: "Purgation, illumination, contemplation"—the three stages of the Via Mystica, acknowledged by all the masters who had trod it, the explorers who had left notes of its geography behind. This trinity of experience seemed to co-relate in some way with the triune vision of reality—"The triple star of goodness, truth, and beauty"—promised to those who attained its highest stage. In his wanderings, apparently so devious, he had followed the old lines very exactly. He looked back on his feverish years; his poor efforts to grasp some detail of the shadow show as it passed him, and make it real for himself.

⌇

Looking into the depths of the woods, seeing against white sky strong trunks and wandering branches all laced together in a mysterious friendship, nothing is easier than to believe in nymphs, dryads, elemental presences of the forest. They stand shadowy upon the paths; they laugh and sigh; and sometimes the soul hears them with a sudden terror. Paganism is thrust upon one in the country; a whole invisible, immemorial population walks upon the lonely heaths and makes the brushwood tremble. It cries, "You come with your new beliefs; your religions, dragged from the East and seated in the heavens; your science, and your blinded common sense; and deny us. But we—we looked out on Arthur's knights, to us the old Romans came in fear and in secret; we are of the earth all-powerful and intangible. You cannot touch us, and we cannot die. All is of the earth; the teeming spirit-world is her breath, pervading all and seen of none. You speak to us of a Christ who came from the heavens. We say no, he came from the earth. The sum of her pure impulses and poetic forces, her power for a magical righteousness, reached their term in him. He is the fair Brother of whom the dark creatures of the forests know dimly; as Jacob and Esau, so Pan and Christ. Both live. But do not fling back the terrible birth on earth's bosom, and deny her her beautiful Son. Look back, and see how many times she has strained toward the ideal which he perfected; see the Buddha births, the fair god of the Norsemen, Phœbus Apollo, and the rest. The Incarnation was an incarnation of earth-holiness, which God gave her with the breath of life when she was made."

In such a way the voices of the woods spoke to Mr. Willie Hopkinson as he trod a path between the trees. He gave them a willing attention. He had developed the sense of adventure; that power which differentiates the romantic from the prosaic world. He felt that everything was possible, and to one who is in this disposition the impossible is sure to come. Want of faith in the improbable is really responsible for all that is deliberately dreary in our lives. Those who go whistling down the road, eyes raised to the sun and hope waiting round the corner, seldom find the excursion of a life a disappointing one.

EARLY WRITINGS

3 Quoted in Margaret Cropper, *Life of Evelyn Underhill* (New York: Harper & Collins, 1958), 5-6.

5 Evelyn Underhill, *The Gray World* (The Century Co., 1904), 35–41; 104–112, 250–52, 321–23.

10 Evelyn Underhill, *Mysticism: The Nature and Development of Spiritual Consciousness* (Oxford: Oneworld Publications 1999), 34–38, 56–62, 104, 125–128, 241–244, 444–51.

43 Quoted in Cropper: *Life of Evelyn Underhill*, 49.

43a Ibid., 51.

44 Evelyn Underhill, *The Mystic Way: The Role of Mysticism in the Christian Life*, (Atlanta: Ariel Press. 1992), 39–56.

63 Quoted in Cropper: *Life of Evelyn Underhill*, 39-40.

APPLIED SPIRITUALITY

65 Evelyn Underhill, *Practical Mysticism*, (New York: E.P. Dutton Co., Inc., 1915), 1–6.

70 Quoted in Cropper: *Life of Evelyn Underhill*, 59-60

71 Ibid., 99-100.

71a Ibid., 102.

72 Ibid., 100-101.

73 "Green Notebook" Quoted in Dana Greene ed. *Fragments from an Inner Life: The Notebooks of Evelyn Underhill* (Harrisburg, PA: Morehouse Publishing, 1933), 35-36.

73a "Green Notebook" Quoted in Greene, *Fragments from an Inner Life*, 36.

74 "Green Notebook" Ibid., 37.

75 "Green Notebook" Ibid., 37-38.

75a "Green Notebook" Ibid., 39-40.

75b "Green Notebook" Ibid., 40–42.

76 Quoted in Cropper: *Life of Evelyn Underhill*, 105–110.

84a Quoted in Greene, *Fragments from an Inner Life*, 47.

84b Quoted in Ibid., 47.

85c Quoted in Ibid., 48.

86 Evelyn Underhill, *The Essentials of Mysticism and Other Essays*, (Oxford: Oneworld Publications, 1995), 121–138.

101 Quoted in Greene, *Fragments from an Inner Life*, 54–56.

103 Quoted in Cropper, *Life of Evelyn Underhill*, 128.

104 Quoted in Greene, *Fragments from an Inner Life*, October 31, 1923, 56– 58.

105 Evelyn Underhill, *The Ways of the Spirit*, (New York, Crossroads Publishing Company, 1990), 55-56.

106 Ibid., 71–75.

113 Ibid., 77–81.

119 Ibid., 135–139.

125 Quoted in Greene, *Fragments from an Inner Life*, 60-61.

126a Quoted in Ibid., 62.

126b Quoted in Ibid., 65-66.

UNDERSTANDING MYSTICISM

131 Evelyn Underhill, *Mystics of the Church*, (Harrisburg, PA: Morehouse Publishing, 1988), 34.

132 Quoted in Greene, *Fragments from an Inner Life*, 75–77.

134 Evelyn Underhill, *Concerning the Inner Life*, (Oxford: Oneworld Publications, 1999), 16, 21-22, 31–33, 39-40, 45–67 edited.

149 Quoted in Greene, *Fragments from an Inner Life*, 78–81.

153 Quoted in Ibid., 82–84.

156 Underhill, *The Essentials of Mysticism and Other Essays*, 187–196.

MATURE INSIGHT

167 Quoted in Greene, *Fragments from an Inner Life*, 93.

167 Quoted in Cropper, *Life of Evelyn Underhill*, 181–82, 184.

THE SPIRITUAL LIFE

169 Evelyn Underhill, *The Spiritual Life*, (Harrisburg, PA: Morehouse Publishing, 1988), 11–36, 107–123 edited.

184 Quoted in Greene, *Fragments from an Inner Life*, 101.

185 Evelyn Underhill, *Worship*, (Surrey, UK: Eagle Publishing, 1991), 3–8, 85–87, 140.

195 Quoted in Greene, *Fragments from an Inner Life*, 103.

196 Evelyn Underhill, *The Mystery of Sacrifice: A Meditation in the Liturgy*, (Harrisburg, PA: Morehouse Publishing, 1990), 44–51.

202a Quoted in Cropper: *Life of Evelyn Underhill*, 227.

202b Quoted in Ibid., 224, 227.

204 Evelyn Underhill, *Abba*, compiled by Roger L. Roberts, (Harrisburg, PA: Morehouse Publishing, 1982), 8–14, 23–30.

212a Quoted in Cropper: *Life of Evelyn Underhill*, 227.

212b Quoted in Ibid., 231-32.

214 Underhill, *The Essentials of Mysticism and Other Essays*, 36–38.

* *A centuries-old feat by Indian fakirs that impressed foreign visitors. A mango seed was planted in front of the audience and shown at frequent intervals to have sprouted and grown. The magician hollowed the large seed and placed the pliable plant inside.*

The following books are listed in the order in which they appear in this book. Every effort has been made to research, identify, and credit the copyright holder for each title; however, there may still be inadvertent errors. If you should find one, kindly contact Paraclete Press.

Life of Evelyn Underhill, by Margaret Cropper. New York: Harper & Brothers, Publishers, 1958.

The Gray World, by Evelyn Underhill. The Century Co., 1904. Used by permission of the Estate of Evelyn Underhill.

Mysticism: The Nature and Development of Spiritual Consciousness, by Evelyn Underhill. Oxford: Oneworld Publications, 1999. Used by permission of the publisher.

The Mystic Way: The Role of Mysticism in the Christian Life, by Evelyn Underhill. Atlanta: Ariel Press, 1992. First published in 1913.

Practical Mysticism, by Evelyn Underhill. New York: E.P. Dutton Co., Inc., 1915. Copyright 1991 Eagle Publishing Ltd, 6 Kestrel House, Mill Street, Trowbridge, BA14 8BE. United Kingdom. Used by permission of Eagle Publishing.

Fragments from an Inner Life: The Notebooks of Evelyn Underhill, edited by Dana Greene. Harrisburg, PA: Morehouse Publishing, 1993. Copyright 1993 by Dana Greene. Used by permission of the editor.

The Essentials of Mysticism and Other Essays, by Evelyn Underhill. Oxford: Oneworld Publications, 1995. Used by permission of the publisher.

The Ways of the Spirit, by Evelyn Underhill. New York: The Crossroad Publishing Company, 1990. Used by permission of the publisher.

The Mystics of the Church, by Evelyn Underhill. Harrisburg, PA: Morehouse Publishing, 1988. Used by permission of the Estate of Evelyn Underhill.

Concerning the Inner Life, by Evelyn Underhill. Oxford: Oneworld Publications, 1999. Used by permission of the publisher.

The Spiritual Life, by Evelyn Underhill. Harrisburg, PA: Morehouse Publishing, 1984. Originally published by Mowbray, a Continuum imprint,1984. Used by permission of the Estate of Evelyn Underhill.

Worship, by Evelyn Underhill. Copyright 1991 Eagle Publishing Ltd, 6 Kestrel House, Mill Street, Trowbridge, BA14 8BE. United Kingdom. Used by permission of Eagle Publishing.

The Mystery of Sacrifice: A Meditation in the Liturgy, by Evelyn Underhill. Harrisburg, PA: Morehouse Publishing, 1990. Originally published by Longmans, Green and Co., LTD, 1938. Used by permission of the Estate of Evelyn Underhill.

Abba, by Evelyn Underhill, compiled by Roger L. Roberts. Harrisburg, PA: Morehouse Publishing, 1982. Orinally published by Mowbray, a Continuum imprint,1981. Used by permission of the Estate of Evelyn Underhill.